==

=======

Spiritual Parenting

Renewing the Hearts of Leaders

Dr. LeAndrew (Lee) Tyson, Sr.

ISBN: 978-0-578-61138-9

Unless otherwise indicated, all Scriptures are taken
from the

King James Version of the Bible

Printed in the U.S.A. by:

Lulu Publishers
1-844-212-0689

Foreword

I could not be more honored to write the foreword for Spiritual Parenting:

Renewing the Hearts of Leaders. Dr. Lee Tyson, my dear friend, and co-laborer in the faith has given the body of Christ a must-read guideline for entering and maximizing true spiritual parenting. Dr. Tyson's writing style reveals both his depth of experience and passion he brings to the subject of spiritual mentoring, coaching, and leadership.

Because I know my friend, I am fully persuaded that the Lord placed a deep burden on Dr. Tyson's heart to address the leadership abuse within the church by presenting God's original plan for spiritual servant leadership. Spiritual Parenting: Renewing the Hearts of Leaders covers the entire scope of spiritual parenting. Dr. Tyson begins his book with the need for spiritual parenting and takes the reader on a beautiful journey through the twists and turns of making bad decisions as a parent or child and then culminates with proper adjustments within the parent/child relationship that results in one of the greatest joys in life: watching the ministry of the child exceed the work of the parent!

There is no better time than now for Dr. Lee Tyson's book to be released to the body of Christ. I have personally encountered countless numbers of men and women leaders who have either been abused by leadership or lack the biblical information concerning seeking, entering and releasing in spiritual parenting.

I thank the Lord for raising up Dr. Lee Tyson to provide the godly guidelines for those who are seeking spiritual parenting and accountability.

Apostle Jerome Steele

Amazing Grace Christian Center

Acknowledgments

No acknowledgment is proper or adequate without first acknowledging the guiding source for all spiritual accomplishment, and that is the Lord Jesus Christ, without whom, I am incomplete, inadequate, and most miserable. I am thankful for the relentless prompting of His Holy Spirit to do this project.

I am thankful for the countless people whom I have met over the years, including my spiritual children who did not cease to inquire about either the availability of or the writing of my book. Chief among them Bishop Tim Holden and other the sons and daughters who pushed me off the fence of procrastination to get this book out to the body of Christ.

I am thankful for my biological children and their willingness to share me with the kingdom and embrace the assignment for my life.

I am thankful to my great friend, Apostle Jerome Steele for being a natural spiritual coach with his constant infusion of revelatory wisdom that could only come from God. He has been the epitome of a true friend, because, he had been consistent even during the trying times.

I am thankful for Pastors Dwight and Princess Dobbins and the New Way Ministries family for setting a standard of excellence that would not allow me to even attempt to publish anything that did not strive to achieve excellence.

I am thankful for Apostles Pernell Applewhite and Phillip Jenkins for the incredible leadership that they are providing for our national ministry that afforded me the time and peace of mind to finish this project.

I am thankful for Keyon (Moneka) Patterson and Fred (Chasity) Jacobs for their constant encouragement and support. As well as Pastor Frankie (Yolanda) Bootie and Bishop Charles (Martha) Runnels for their support of our ministry for years.

I certainly thank God for my spiritual parents Apostle Lionel and Lady Jeanette Childress who constantly inspire me to achieve and the love that they and their family and the CCI Fellowship show me and my family and ministry.

And last but by no means least, I want to thank my wife Joann who has been my chief cheerleader, encourager, intercessor, love of my life, and most of all; my best friend. She has been my daily inspiration in life and ministry and has sacrificed so much to be the wife and partner of a passionate visionary. She has not only allowed but has encouraged my creativity even when it has gone against the grain. I am so thankful that she trusts God in me.

Preface

This book has been incubating in my spirit since I was born into this world. One of the most difficult things that I have encountered in my life has been to develop the discipline that it takes to work on a book project consistently. I have started and stopped so many books in the past that I almost lost the desire to write, even though I have always known that I have a mandate to write books to enhance the lives of believers. I have been so engrossed in procrastination that I have used "too busy" to camouflage it. Thank God, that the need to write this book became greater than any excuse not to.

One of the most hurtful things that I have noticed as I have traveled evangelistically is the lack of either spiritual parenting or proper spiritual parenting. One of the most successful strategies in business is to recognize a demand and then develop a strategy to supply it. Countless fortunes have been made by employing this key business principle. Sadly though, the body of Christ has not recognized this as an effective ministry tool. There is great need; however; there is both a small demand and even smaller availability of supply.

Two extreme camps currently exist in the body of Christ, and both are numerous. There is the camp that does not believe that it needs any guidance at all, and they conclude that the Holy Spirit is all that is needed for successful ministry.

There is another camp that recognizes the need for accountability and guidance but, is willing to settle for any entity professing to provide such, even if that entity is unaccountable itself.

For this reason, the Spirit of God has been relentless even to the point of disrupting a sound sleep to get me to get this resource out to the Body. The catalyst for my passion for this matter comes from 1 Corinthians 4:14-15, when Paul says I do not write this to shame you, but to warn and counsel you as my beloved children. After all, though you should have ten thousand teachers (guides to direct you) in Christ, yet you do not have many fathers, For, I became your father in Christ Jesus through the gospel (amplified).

My prayer is that the readers will get as much comfort from this book, as I have gotten in researching material, and writing it. There is some necessary redundancy, due to certain Scriptures and expressions being relevant in different chapters.

Table of Contents

Chapter 1

Recognizing the Need for Spiritual Parenting

God did not create humans to live alone. The Scripture says that He created male and female and told them to be fruitful, multiply, and fill the earth, thus indicating procreation. Therefore, it is necessary to understand, that procreation brings about a parent and child relationship. It is the responsibility of the parent to nurture, guide, and protect the offspring that comes forth as the result of procreation. It is in this same light that I believe we must look at spiritual parent/child relationships, so that the child has the benefit of the assignment of the parents, and the parents have fulfillment in completing that assignment.

One of the most needed gifts in the body of Christ; ironically is also the most forsaken, and that is the gift of spiritual fathers with the heart of a faithful father. The body is inundated with spiritual fathers in name, but few in the heart. The 20th Century produced a multitude of denominations, organizations, reformations, fellowships, and many other entities that allowed many in ministry to come into covenant connections. These connections were supposedly for the sake of accountability and ministry support. Of these entities, people refer to the leading figures as "Spiritual Fathers or Spiritual Mothers." To the dismay of many disillusioned followers; what was advertised and what was presented were not the same.

What was supposed to be a father or mother, too often was nothing more than egomaniacal, eccentric or tyrannical individuals, whose sole motivation was (and is) to exert power over the lives of those who joined them. In many cases, the expected worship of the leading figure exceeds the worship of Jesus, and anything less than absolute loyalty to the leader was (and is) considered traitorous and almost blasphemous. The only people who are enhanced (mostly financially) under this type of regime, are the leading figures themselves, while the son or daughter is more deficient in direction than when they first connected.

I have found in most cases, that the leaders mentioned above lacked the aid of spiritual parenting themselves, and it is difficult for them to be what they had never been properly groomed to be. If one does not have either a father or the right father (mother where applicable), it is difficult to be a father or the right father. What remains is self-taught leadership, without the benefit of checks and balances. When someone attempts to lead where they have never been, they misdirect others on their journeys.

True fathers were once true sons (daughters where applicable). The knowledge and wisdom gained from that relationship gives proper preparation to become what your son-ship grooms you for, and that is a father with the son's best interest in mind. That is because as a son, you have the father's best interest in mind, and the seed of son-ship produces the harvest of fatherhood. The father is what a former son was elevated to, with the same understanding that the essence of both levels is servitude.

The heart of a faithful father, is filled with the understanding that to fulfill the mandate to get the son to the destination of his assignment, requires serving the son, simultaneously as the son is serving (more on this in a later chapter). Dr. Jonason Pack has an excellent book on son-ship called "Son-ship: The Strategy of Submission," that positions sons in the selection pool from which fathers are taken. He brings out the essence of a son that should produce the strength and wisdom of a father.

If the son does not exceed the father in most areas of ministry; one of two things has happened, either the father failed him, or the son did not heed the wisdom of the father. It should be very difficult to exceed the wisdom of a father because what you need in a father should increase as your need increases. The source increases as the need increases.

I sought a spiritual father for the greatest part of my ministry, and because I have understood accountability and submission, I refused to be uncovered. That led to my being submitted under the types of leaders described earlier and some cases submitting to leaders that could not provide what I needed because they didn't have it. That led to years of such futility, and I vowed never to be a leader that produced futility in another minister's life.

When the Lord brought my true spiritual father into my life, I heard his voice before I saw his face, and my spirit leaped in the same way that John leaped in Elizabeth's womb, when she encountered a mutually pregnant Mary. I knew that this was the voice that I had been listening for my entire life and I did not hesitate to make it known. Apostle Lionel Childress, Sr. is the epitome of a spiritual father in that he has the combination of a powerful anointing, wisdom beyond comprehension, extremely gifted preacher and prophet, but also genuine humility and love unfeigned. He also has the drive to see his spiritual children do the greater works. His example is the model for the type of father that I have always strived to be. It has been through my connection with this powerful man of God, that I have become even better at what I have always been pretty good doing.

I will accept nothing less than my sons excelling in their ministries, as well as exceeding what I have done in ministry and life. The ability to ensure that this is a reality is certainly more probable now that my ability to do so has been enhanced by my access to the faithfulness of my father's heart. A true father relishes the success of his children rather than feel inferior by it. In no way are you demeaned as a father when your children exceed your accomplishments or boundaries. To the contrary, it says volumes about the parent/child relationship, because the father was

6

willing to guide, and the child was willing to follow the guidance.

True fathers are always in search mode to discover and pioneer areas that the child is to go into, to lessen the difficulties of their getting there; when necessary. Some adverse experiences, can enhance the child to become more equipped to deal with the difficulties of life, more than the father trying to prevent every adverse experience. Sometimes the value of an experience is not realized until one must pay for it, as opposed to every solution being given. The skill of the father is to recognize when the situation presents the opportunity to provide the solution for it (if indeed he has it), or to allow the child to find the solution based on lessons already learned.

The primary responsibilities of even biological fathers are to produce, train, guide, and monitor their children's lives. One of the most misquoted and misused scriptures in the Bible is Proverbs 13:22 that says "a good man leaves an inheritance to his children's children: and the wealth of the sinner is laid up for the just. The church norm has been to present this solely as a financial mantra. That has done more to create a covetous generation of waiting for what belongs to someone else, as opposed to looking at the deeper implications that reveal an understanding of moral responsibility.

The amplified Bible illustrates my point: A good man leaves an inheritance [of moral stability and goodness] to his children's children, and the wealth of the sinner [finds its way eventually] into the hands of the righteous, for whom it was laid up. That shows that first, the good man is a father with vision because he is looking at the immediate father/son relationship with another generation in mind. The implication is that the son's children should benefit from the son's experiences, just as he is benefitting from his father's experiences. Note also, that the responsibility to teach moral responsibility, as well as giving wisdom and guidance comes before the mention of wealth, because fiscal responsibility without moral responsibility is a recipe for disaster. For what profit a man to gain the whole world and lose his soul.

The heart of a faithful father is filled with the desire to see his children in a position to hear the words that all of God's people long to hear, and that is "well done thy good and faithful servant." That takes a commitment, to see every step in the process through to the very end. One of the greatest hindrances to the fulfillment of anything is allowing either distractions or obstacles to cause one to put off until tomorrow what should be completed today Then. tomorrow begets tomorrow to the extent that the whatever it is that should have been completed, becomes dormant.

Spiritual parenting does not just benefit the son or the daughter; it also benefits the father, in more ways than one. Psalms 68:19 says that God loads us daily with benefits. The mistake that most people make is in thinking that the benefits that we are loaded with are exclusively for us. That line of thinking is in contrast with the structure of God's kingdom because we are designed to be in constant help mode.

The Lord spoke to Abram in Genesis 12:2 that He (God) would bless him and that he would be a blessing. The benefits that we are daily loaded with take on an added significance when we apply it to spiritual parenting because our greatest benefits are more directly tied to our assignments to complete our spiritual children.

Dr. Myles Monroe was often quoted as saying that "the wealthiest place on earth is the cemetery," because of all the ideas that people take to the grave with them that should have been shared in life.

The parent needs the child as much as the child needs the parent because, without a child, it is difficult to be a plausible parent. Therein lies another problem in the Body; we have allowed spiritual foster parenting to replace direct spiritual

10

parenting, because of the shortage of willing spiritual parents. Abram said to the Lord in Genesis 15:3; "behold, you have given me no offspring, and a member of my household will be my heir (Esv)." In other words, I have no plausibility as a parent because I do not have the benefit of having sired a child, so I am in the position of being a foster father to my servant.

Now I know that there are some circumstances where a person is unable to produce a child for whatever reason. However, there is never a time that a person in the spirit is forced to be childless because there are countless thousands of men and women in search of spiritual parenting. Some have been orphaned, others have been simply abandoned because of the inability to connect with their spiritual parent. The most tragic situation that has spiritual children in need of spiritual parenting is abuse. Abuse from leaders is nothing new. However, it has taken on epic proportions in the church today.

When the true fathers and mothers step up and take their positions in the kingdom and begin to receive and embrace those children whom God has mandated for them to nurture, protect, and train; then the Body of Christ will become a force to be reckoned with. Jesus visualized this force when He told Peter in Matthew 16:18; "upon this rock, I will build My church, and the gates of Hades (the powers of the infernal region) shall not overpower it [or be strong to its detriment or hold out against it] (amp).

That shows, that the inability of the gates of hell to prevent the advancement of the church of Jesus Christ is from a defensive position and not an offensive position. One of the responsibilities of the spiritual parent is to differentiate the defensive and the offensive abilities of the body of Christ so that we are not binding what we should loose and loosing what we should be binding. This responsibility cannot be carried out if there is no parent/child relationship in which to do so. Prayerfully, none of the readers of this book from a son or daughter perspective are being offended by the term child or spiritual child. Jesus said in Luke 18:17 that "whoever does not receive the kingdom of God like a child shall not enter it." The strength of the parent/child relationship is properly distinguishing the roles of the relationship and understanding the duties therein.

Humanity could neither have existed nor continue to exist without parents to reproduce the species. Conversely, the kingdom of God cannot exist as a legitimate kingdom, without spiritual parents positioning their spiritual children, to do unto others what has been done unto them to assure their assignments' fulfillment (more on this in a later chapter). There is far too much illegitimacy operating in the kingdom currently (as it relates to authorized spiritual parents), and the body of Christ has taken on the character of the world, where babies are producing babies. Again, this is happening either because children have not found that spiritual parent, or are not seeking a spiritual parent, because they feel no need to have one.

To reverse this trend, spiritual parents must avail themselves like never before. I firmly believe, that renewing of the hearts of leaders to give themselves to spiritual parenting, will be met proportionately, by renewed hearts of children to be parented. Now there are some spiritual children whose hearts need no renewing; what they need is renewed hope of spiritual parents being available to them.

The essence of the heart of a faithful father is that it is magnetic and draws to it the sons and daughters for whom the Lord forms the hearts. It is not that the body has been void of faithful hearted fathers; it is that they have been so few in numbers. There are thousands, and probably millions of individuals with fatherhood capacities, however, there are not remotely enough with the necessary hearts to be fathers. That is in no small part due to the declining recognition of the necessity of the relationships, particularly from many leader's perspectives.

14

When the focus is more numerical in scope than nutritional for the enhancement of the process, the result is a preference of quantity over quality and mistaking them for the same. Thankfully, there is enough of a remnant of faithful hearted fathers to sustain the hope of the renewing of the hearts of others with fatherhood capacities, to embrace the challenge of spiritual parenting and its authenticity. When we approach spiritual parenting with a commitment to wholeheartedly provide the nourishment that our spiritual children need; we will leave such an indelible mark on their lives, that their greatest desires will be to ensure that they provide others with what has been provided for them.

Chapter 2

Understanding the God Factor

One of the most critical mistakes made in spiritual parenting (whether choosing a spiritual parent or receiving and embracing a spiritual child) is doing so without the wisdom and guidance of the Lord. That is happening far too often, and more times than not it; leads to exploitive relationships, whether the parent is exploiting the child or vice versa. I suppose that it has always been, however; of late you find more people connecting in spiritual parenting relationship, more to enhance their chances of gaining prominence and national platforms, than for forming a mentor/mentee relationship.

There is more of a parasitic agenda from the child rather than a protégé relationship, and the

16

child seeks more of what the man has earned than what the mentor has learned. The other side of that equation is; that there are those that disguise themselves as mentors, and they have a leech agenda. They seek to drain the unsuspecting mentee of his or her resources, and leave them destitute, before moving on to the next victim of their godless quests.

If God is the driving force behind the connection, the relationship can be long and fruitful. The Lord gives His word in this because He said in Jeremiah 3:15, "I will give you [spiritual] shepherds after My own heart [in the final time], who will feed you with knowledge and understanding *and* judgment (amp)." Not only does God give us spiritual parents after His own heart; He also fills them with the wisdom and the knowledge that is needed to propel us into our kingdom assignments.

What we must understand is that, even though He equips parents with everything that the child will need, He doesn't release it in them all at once. That is to avoid the tendency of getting what you need, and then abandoning the relationship prematurely. God is into lifetime relationships, and even after the child has grown into and is entrenched in his assignment, there will always be the need, to periodically go back to the parent for wisdom for a difficult situation. That helps the parent, to stay fruitful with wisdom, regardless of age.

As long as your true spiritual parent lives, he will always be equipped with fruit for you. A foster parent will run out of things to give you because they are limited in what they have for you. Many of us have been in a foster relationship before, where the foster parent admittedly gave us all that they could give us, so they released us to seek that spiritual parent who could take us further. On the other hand, the mentality of that true parent is, there is more from where that came.

Mature spiritual parents know within themselves whether they are foster parents, or God prepared parents. Whether they know it according to this terminology or not, they know when they have exhausted their capacity to release what the spiritual child needs, and do not feel inadequate, when that capacity is reached. The foster parent knows that when that capacity has been reached, it is time to release the child; the true parent, knows that a refill of resources is imminent.

This assessment of types of spiritual parentage is by no means meant to diminish the importance of the foster parent. Foster parents have within them, sustainable wisdom to supply you until you connect with that parent you have needed, and hopefully in pursuit of. The thing about a foster parent is that they are the actual spiritual parent of someone; just not you. Therefore, they have the heart of a parent and will guide you in ways of wisdom, so that, your God sanctioned parent, does not have to deprogram you. The one thing that you never want to do is to be mandated with an assignment from the Lord, and not be accountable anywhere.

We must be mindful, that prayerfully seeking the Lord for that spiritual parent, is no different than prayerfully seeking Him for anything else; He doesn't always answer immediately. The Lord often puts us in position, for us to discover what we have in us, and what we are to do with the information when we discover it. Then he connects us with those parents whom He has chosen for us to refine what we have.

Many times, the Lord will leave us seemingly on an island in our quest for that spiritual parent, for us to get the wisdom of accountability. That is so that when we do connect with that spiritual parent, we don't make their assignment a burdensome task, because we either don't fully grasp the concept of accountability, or we refuse to be accountable. In situations like these, even foster parents are not revealed unto us. When we find ourselves in that island situation, it is far better to connect with a brother on your level, who has your best interest at heart than not to be connected at all. Because, even though that brother cannot do anything to get you to that next phase of your assignment, at least they can help you to avoid losing any ground. Just be careful not to substitute a peer for a parent.

The greatest benefit in seeking God for that spiritual parent, who is so necessary, for the success and longevity of your ministry, is that God not only knows where you are designated to be, He also knows who can help you to get there. Just like He created you for your assignment to others, He created someone else, whose assignment is you. In His omniscience, God knows everything that we will ever need, to do everything that we have been called to do, and He knows who to deposit those resources into for your benefit, and that person is more than willing, to mentor, protect, and guide you into your destiny.

It is critical however, that when the Lord leads us to that person, that we don't miss them, because they don't physically, financially, or articulately, fit the profile of what we thought that our parent should resemble. That has led to the downfall of many men and women of God; seeking spiritual parentage, because many have been beguiled by what the supposed parent appeared to possess, and have lost ministry, possessions, and some even their lives. Do not get caught in the trap of external expectations when it is internal revelations that you need. Just because they don't look the part does not mean that they are not who you need.

It must be understood, that there are people out there who are misrepresenting the kingdom of God, solely or the purpose of prestige, and control over the lives of others. They will do or say anything to get you to believe that they are sent from the Lord, to guide your destiny. Though I am a spiritual father to many sons and daughter, I never have been, and will not become a recruiter of ministers, regardless of what I see, concerning their destinies. Kingdom assignments are too vital and valuable to misdirect anyone merely for personal gain.

There is a story in 1 Kings 13, that reveals the detriment of disobeying the voice of God, simply because there seems to be a more experienced ministry gift, encouraging you to do so. This young prophet had been sent by the Lord, to cry against the altar of Jeroboam, to the behest of the king. When the king tried to have the young man seized, the hand that he pointed toward him, dried up and became paralyzed. At the kings pleading to the young man for prayer for his hand, the young man prayed, and the king's hand was restored.

King Jeroboam invited the young man to go with him so that the young man could be refreshed. The young man refused because he had been instructed by the Lord, not to eat, drink, or go home with anyone. But look at how the story turns, when a seemingly more experienced prophet comes into the picture. Now an old prophet lived in Bethel. And his sons came and told him all that the man of God had done that day in Bethel. They also said to their father the words that he had spoken to the king. And their father said to them, "Which way did he go?" And his sons showed him the way that the man of God who came from Judah had gone. And he said to his sons, "Saddle the donkey for me." So, they saddled the donkey for him, and he mounted it.

And he went after the man of God and found him sitting under an oak. And he said to him, "Are you the man of God who came from Judah?" And he said, "I am." Then he said to him, "Come home with me and eat bread." And he said, "I may not return with you, or go in with you, neither will I eat bread nor drink water with you in this place, for it was said to me by the word of the LORD, 'You shall neither eat bread nor drink water there, nor return by the way that you came.'" And he said to him, "I also am a prophet as you are, and an angel spoke to me by the word of the LORD, saying, 'Bring him back with you into your house that he may eat bread and drink water.'" But he lied to him.

So, he went back with him and ate bread in his house and drank water. And as they sat at the table, the word of the LORD came to the prophet who had brought him back. And he cried to the man of God who came from Judah, "Thus says the LORD, 'Because you have disobeyed the word of the LORD and have not kept the command that the LORD, your God, commanded you, but have come back and have eaten bread and drunk water in the place of which he said to you, "Eat no bread and drink no water," your body shall not come to the tomb of your fathers.'" And after he had eaten bread and drunk, he saddled the donkey for the prophet whom he had brought back.

And as he went away, a lion met him on the road and killed him. And his body was thrown in the road, and the donkey stood beside it; the lion also stood beside the body. And behold, men passed by and saw the body was thrown in the road and the lion standing by the body. And they came and told it in the city where the old prophet lived. And when the prophet who had brought him back from the way heard of it, he said, "It is the man of God who disobeyed the word of the LORD; therefore, the LORD has given him to the lion, which has torn him and killed him, according to the word that the LORD spoke to him."

That shows that the old prophet truly could see who this young man was in the Lord. He should have either stayed out of his way altogether or encouraged the young man to obey the instructions of the Lord. However, he did neither and contributed to the death of this young man. How many times, have men and women of God been in the position, to be given spiritual insight into the assignment of a young man or woman in ministry, and should have either stayed out of their way (as they were seeking their spiritual parent), or should have encouraged them to obey the Lord's instructions? And how many young men and women, have lost all, because they disobeyed the voice of God, and acquiesced to the lies of a man or a woman.

Though I use young man or woman for the sake of correlating the story, to the reality of what is happening in the kingdom; many men and women are entering the ministry at late stages of their lives and are just as vulnerable to the deceptions of self-serving leaders. That is why the God factor is so critical in connecting in a spiritual parenting relationship.

I have heard people, go so far as to say that they sought the Lord in what they would wear; in what they would drive, and where they would live, but did not seek Him before connecting with a spiritual parent. I don't think that it matters much to God as to where you live; as it does to Him for how you live. Likewise, He's probably not overly concerned about what you wear or drive. However, it does matter to Him, who you submit your life to, and that is where He truly needs to be consulted.

One can attend any of the numerous Holy Convocations, or some other official reformation's, organization's, or demonization's event, and find people immaculately dressed, but miserable in countenance because they do not fit in where they are trying to. I am sure, that many of them asked the Lord what to wear, what to give, and how to respond to an unmerited rebuke from a tyrannical leader, but they did not seek the Lord, on how to disconnect themselves from an unfruitful alliance, and they have spent time and money to be miserable.

The blame for these unfruitful alliances does not rest squarely on the shoulders of the leaders in these relationships, because when the spiritual relationship is done correctly, it is the child seeking God for the parent, and the parent seeking God for the wisdom to guide the child. Therefore, if the child allowed himself or herself to be recruited, instead of being directed; they must share the blame for the outcome. Self-serving people seek to serve themselves, so no one should be mystified when they do what they are accustomed to doing. It should be both expected and avoided.

God will never lead us astray. We might find ourselves astray; however, it was not God who put us in that position. Somehow, we violated the rule of Scripture, leaned to our understanding, and ended up in a place that is foreign, to the place that God had in mind for us. That is not to say, that the Lord will never lead us into some uncomfortable places. There are times that He will do so to reveal Himself as the God of our rescue from that place, and to show us that truly, all things work together for good, for them that love Him, and called according to His purpose.

Whenever we find ourselves in such places of uncomfortableness, our consolation is, that wherever God leads us, He takes full responsibility. We also must see the process as a journey. In other words, many of the places that we find ourselves in, that appeared to have no relevance to our assignments, are merely stopovers. We need never panic and mistake a stopover for a residence. To the contrary, we must see it as a place of rest, regardless of how unappealing it may be.

My biological father worked many years for Greyhound Bus Lines, which allowed us to travel virtually anywhere in the United States. Anyone familiar with traveling by bus knows that a bus makes frequent stops, to pick up and drop off passengers. At some point, it makes what is called a rest stop. Many of these rest stops are very drab and unappealing. Some of them are sometimes attended by unassuming and sometimes even rude people. However, we must keep in mind that the purpose of the rest stop, is not to observe the appearance of the building or to be catered to by customer friendly people, the purpose of the stop, is to stretch your legs and rest.

Because of the limited capacity of the bus, the rest is very difficult while the bus is in motion. Therefore, it is essential to understand that the bus is merely a vehicle, and the journey is merely a process, and the purpose of both is to get you to your destination. That is what God wants us to see, relating to the process of our spiritual journey. We may not always enjoy the ride, and the places of rest may not be the most appealing. However, we must remember that it is all a process to get us to our destination. The ride is much easier when we use the God factor, to make the trip.

Chapter 3

Understanding Mutual Servitude

In the kingdom of God, there is but one throne, and that throne is to be occupied by God alone, and if there is a pedestal, that is reserved for Him also. That is a truth that seems to be lost on many leaders, because everything about them is to be served by those whom they lead. There are far more cultic relationships in the body of Christ than most care to admit. Throughout the body, there are one man ruled organizations, to the extent that one man controls every facet of the people's lives under their administration.

It is viewed as blasphemous to refer to them by any name other than their title. More attention is given to them than to the word of God, and this is often due to the total misapplication of Scripture. There an expectation of blind loyalty where nothing is questioned and the leader for all practical intents and purposes is lord over the people. That is contrary to what Jesus taught because He (being God in human flesh) said in Matthew 20:28 that He did not come to be served, but to serve.

The factors that have contributed to the lack of servitude in the body of Christ are many. There is such a negative perception of servitude (because in the eyes of many it has a slave connotation). Also, neither the parent nor the child has conceptualized the benefit of servitude. In some cases, servitude is seen as a threat to one's lordship. To fully grasp the necessity of servitude, it is important to address the factors that contribute to a lack thereof. Jesus showed how servitude is not the worst thing that a leader can do, but the best thing. This scenario takes place and Mark chapter 10 when the disciples were jockeying for an internal position. Beginning at verse 35, this is how the scenario unfolds.

Then James and John, the sons of Zebedee, came to Him, saying, "Teacher, we want you to do for us whatever we ask." And He said to them, "What do you want Me to do for you?" They said to Him, "Grant us that we may sit, one on your right hand and the other on your left, in your glory." But Jesus said to them, "You do not know what you ask. Are you able to drink the cup that I drink, and be baptized with the baptism that I am baptized with?" They said to Him, "We are able." So, Jesus said to them, "You will indeed drink the cup that I drink, and with the baptism, I am baptized with you will be baptized; but to sit on My right hand and on My left is not Mine to give, but *it is for those* for whom it is prepared."

And when the ten heard *it,* they began to be greatly displeased with James and John. But Jesus called them to Himself and said to them, "You know that those who are considered rulers over the Gentiles lord it over them, and their great one's exercise authority over them. Yet it shall not be so among you, but whoever desires to become great among you shall be your servant. And whoever of you desires to be first shall be slave of all. He further illustrates

His point in Matthew 20:28, "for even the Son of Man did not come to be served, but to serve, and to give His life a ransom for many." The word slave is from the Greek word: "doulos," which means a bondsman or a man of servile condition. The metaphor is one who gives himself up to another's will those whose service is used by Christ in extending and advancing his cause among men. It also means a servant.

A servant must not be looked upon as an unwilling participant; to the contrary, he is a willing slave to the assignment that God has given him to guide another to the fulfillment of his assignment. So then, even if the perception of a servant is one of slaves, it must not be a negative perception. Because God has deemed this level of commitment necessary in the spiritual parent/child relationship.

The fact that Jesus is the orchestrator of the concept of the greatest among you being the slave of all should be enough to apply one's self to serving. If we have learned anything from the word of God, it is that there has always been a great benefit in obeying God. The Bible goes so far as to say that to obey, is better than sacrifice (1 Samuel 15:22). There are countless incidences throughout the entire word of God that identify benefits in obeying the Lord's instructions.

Servitude is such a part of the nature of true leaders; that it is almost grievous and certainly unfulfilling to them when they do not have an opportunity to serve. They realize that what is burning inside them does not belong to them, and there is little peace until they allowed to release it. They also understand that the release of the gift inside of them is mutually beneficial because there is just as much joy in releasing what one has for another, as there is for the recipient of the release. Paul makes a powerful statement to that effect in Romans 1:11-12 when he said "for I long to see you, that I may impart to you some spiritual gift, so that you may be established, that is, that I may be encouraged together with you by the mutual faith both of you and me. He shows how one entrenched in servitude is encouraged they can serve others.

That is the opposite for those who see leadership as lordship because their mentality is to be served rather than to serve. For this type of leader; to serve (in their mind), threatens their throne. It is essential to their ego to be in control of everything and everyone, and anything contrary to this is not to be tolerated. The nature of these leaders is usually extremely volatile and unpredictable. They take great delight in belittling people (especially in crowds of people) to show that they are in charge. That type of leader is not a leader whom God has chosen to be either an equipped spiritual parent or a beneficial foster parent. That is someone who took advantage of either unsuspecting or undiscerning people and presented themselves as something that they were not and put themselves in a leadership position.

They leave trails of wounded, broken, and battered people, who are difficult to develop for the true assignments that God has for them. Because, their trust is often broken, and they carry fragments of the abusive leader. They tend to expect some resemblance of the abusive leader for another spiritual parent to be authentic in their lives. Even though the abusive treatment is wrong, it becomes accepted, and normally the reason for their departure from the leader is initiated by the leader, either because the abused had nothing else to offer, or began to show signs of independence. Rarely do they look for anyone to lead them with genuine love and commitment to their success because they have become so conditioned to the abuse. That is a form of the "Stockholm Syndrome," which is defined as an emotional attachment to a captor by a former hostage as a result of continuous stress, dependence, and a need to cooperate for survival.

Men and women of God who have kingdom assignments and have been in abusive relationships with former leaders, rarely have an issue with serving, because that is all that they are accustomed. Their biggest issue is accepting that a leader should serve them, as well. They make statements like, "you shouldn't be doing that," or "I can't let you do that," or other statements of that nature. While it is admirable to desire to lessen the load of your leader, it also must be understood that the leader has as much of a mandate to serve as those whom they lead. Elijah served Elisha by mentoring him continuously, but Elisha was often referred to as the one who washed the hands of Elijah.

Servitude has built in fulfillment. Therefore, it is incumbent for it to be in full operation by the parent and the child. If we are to understand the true essence of the Godhead, we must look at it through the eyes of mutual servitude. The Father serves the Son, by answering the prayers of the people in Son's name, and the Son serves the Father by being the Savior and Lord of His people. God relegates Himself to the dual roles, to show us how mutual servitude is done, and that there is nothing wrong with it. If it is honorable for the godhead to serve mutually; there can be nothing dishonorable in our serving each other.

Proverbs 27:17 says that iron sharpens iron, so a man sharpens the countenance of his friend. That shows mutual benefit in mutual servitude. Ephesians 4:16 puts it this way, the body fitly framed and knit together through that which every joint supply, according to the working in due measure of each several parts, makes the increase of the body unto the building up of itself in love.

That brings another characteristic of a true spiritual parent; they love everything that they do in the relationship, including servitude. That is not to say that they like everything that needs to be done to fulfill their assignment, however, their love of God, and the privilege of being chosen to be a spiritual parent, overrides any dislike during the assignment.

If one kept in mind the golden rule to do unto others as you would have them do unto you, mutual servitude would be automatic. The "a" clause of Proverbs 18:24 says that for a man to have friends, he must show himself friendly. Using that same logic, for a man to be served, he must first serve, and again, that produces mutual servitude. If we look at servitude and approach it from its divine design, we can see that when it is in full implementation, everyone in the world would eventually be served.

A heart of servitude is much more comfortable, and achieves its greatest fulfillment, in giving, rather than receiving. Servitude produces the benevolence of spirit, which is needed to see the needs of others, as opportunities to exhibit the character of Christ in our anthropomorphic interactions. The apostle Paul puts it this way, when the address the elders at Ephesus in acts 20, he said, "In all things I have shown you that by working hard in this way we must help the weak and remember the words of the Lord Jesus, how he said, 'It is more blessed to give than to receive.'" Mutual servitude is beneficial in every segment of society; however, it is essential in a spiritual parenting relationship.

So much more can and needs to be said about mutual servitude. However, it can be addressed in greater detail, when it is the subject matter of an entire book.

Chapter 4

How to Build an Unbreakable Bond

One of the essential parts of life is a relationship. From the beginning of creation, God said it is not good that man should be alone. To understand the relationship, one must also understand the diversity that comes with a relationship. Relationships can be advantageous or disadvantageous, fruitful or fruitless, good or bad, dangerous or safe, etc. It requires the participants and the expectations of the relationship to determine the quality of the relationship.

Relationships are for the most part very joyful and rewarding. However, they can also be very painful and frustrating. That tends to be even more pronounced in spiritual relationships. There is a common saying throughout the body of Christ that there is no hurt like a church hurt. Normally, the hurt that occurs in the church is often at the hands of a leader. However, leaders are hurt far more often than is commonly known. To whomever, the pain is inflicted or by whomever, more times than not it could have been avoided. One of the primary factors that lead to being hurt in the church is the lack of relationship building.

Most people enter relationships with endurance in mind, because people who enter relationships for the right reasons, expect the relationship to endure for a lifetime. One of the greatest hindrances to enduring relationships is not entering the relationship the right way. Many people who got hurt in the spiritual relationships just mentioned, entered for the right reasons, but not the right way. The way to enter every relationship is to enter it the same way that one enters marriage. By that I mean, enter the relationship with a vow of commitment to fulfillment. The commitment is that the relationship will endure through every obstacle that comes against it, no matter what. That is because one enters the relationship with the understanding that this is the relationship that is needed to complete one for his or her assignment in life. This commitment is especially necessary for a spiritual parent/child relationship.

When entering the spiritual parent and spiritual child relationship, both the parent and the child must vow to establish an unbreakable bond. They must be committed to one another, to the extent that they will not allow outside forces to be deterrents to the keeping of the vow. They both realize that God ordained the relationship.

Therefore, just as God says, "what I have joined together, let no man put asunder," referring to marriage, it also must be applied to every relationship that God puts together.

One must not be naïve to think that just because God joins a thing, that what He joins will not face opposition. To the contrary, when God joins a thing, the opposition should be expected, because what God joins, He does so with a mindset of kingdom enhancement. When the enemy recognizes that, is when he formulates his attacks against it. Therefore, it is essential for both the parent and the child to always work toward an agreement.

The agreement ensures that God remains fixed in the relationship. Jesus said Matthew 18:19-20, "if two of you shall agree on earth as touching anything that they shall ask, it shall be done for them of my Father which is in heaven. For where two or three are gathered together in my name, there am I in the midst of them."

When standing on this assurance from the Lord, we lay the foundation for an unbreakable bond. However, the foundation must be built upon using the same thing that the foundation is built with, and that is the word of the Lord.

One of the primary strengthening agents in building an unbreakable bond is loyalty. Loyalty is defined as an unswerving allegiance. To swerve means "to turn aside abruptly from a straight line or course." Therefore, to swerve from the commitment to keep the vows of the relationship, automatically either weakens or destroys the relationship. That normally happens, when one or the other begins to listen to what seems to be more attractive or beneficial than what one has.

I have seen numerous spiritual relationships to be destroyed by the subtlety of the enemy (working through unscrupulous leaders) to project that a spiritual parent is weak and incapable of providing the needs of the spiritual child.

That spirit has created unprecedented chaos throughout the body of Christ, as it relates to spiritual parenting. What has ensued, is spiritual children claiming a multitude of spiritual parents, which has created what I refer to as the "Frankenstein effect." For those unfamiliar with the story, the Frankenstein monster was the creation of a mad scientist's attempt to create a human being from different people's body parts. The most identifiable marks of the monster were the scars that resulted from stitching together body parts from different sources.

That is also what results when one attempts to infuse different personalities, idiosyncrasies, doctrines, etc., into a spiritual son or daughter. Scars are not only inevitable; they will also be quite visible. That is why it is so essential to build unbreakable bonds.

Unbreakable bonds eliminate the ability of the wrong voice to enter into the spirit of the child. It must also be noted that children are not the only ones vulnerable to seductive voices. Many leaders have abandoned their children, to pursue other children offering more to the leader than what the other child was capable.

The ability of another voice to negatively influence a relationship is only possible when the relationship is entered into with ulterior motives. When a relationship is entered for the sole purpose of receiving, when the one from whom they are receiving from ceases to be able to provide, the seeker will seek others to provide, and are incapable of being loyal to anyone but themselves. They leave paths of destruction everywhere they go because of their self-serving agendas.

There is a spiritual truth that is not recognized enough, and that is, a spiritual father or mother, instinctively know the voice of their children, and children instinctively know the voice of their true spiritual parent and will not follow strange voices. Additionally, the spiritual parent/child relationship that God ordains are the only ones that can truly expect for an unbreakable bond to be established and maintained. Though there are exceptions, they are extremely rare, and normally occur as result of a death of another's spiritual parent or child.

Two of the most renowned spiritual parent/child relationships in the Bible are the relationships between Elijah and Elisha, and Paul and Timothy. When we look deeply into these relationships, we can see what established such unbreakable bonds, that they had to be included in the Scriptures. Throughout biblical history, there have possibly been tens of thousands, if not millions of relationships. However, they're not mentioned in Scripture. That should tell us that when a relationship is mentioned in Scripture, it is so important of an example, that it could not be omitted from Scripture.

It is obvious that the relationship between Elijah and Elisha was ordained of God because the Scriptures validates it (1 Kings 19:15). When Elijah was fleeing from the threats of Jezebel, and feeling abandoned, and somewhat self-absorbed (in that he was the only one truly standing for the principles of God), he was given some instructions to anoint certain people for certain tasks.

The Lord told him to anoint Hazael to be king over Syria: and Jehu the son of Nimshi shalt thou anoint to be king over Israel: and Elisha, the son of Shaphat of Abelmeholah shalt thou, anoint to be a prophet in thy room. Hazael and Jehu were anointed to be kings over nations. However, the Elisha was an anointed to become Elijah's successor.

All of these were destined men, as their names indicate. Hazael means "one who sees God," Jehu means "Jehovah is he," and Elisha means "God is salvation." So, if one was to be selected from a godly name alone, and Elijah had been tasked to select his successor, the choice would have been difficult. However, God made a choice for Elijah, which simplified the process, and magnified the relationship.

Elijah's motives had to stay consistent with God's plan. He could very easily have taken advantage of the favor that he had with Hazael and Jehu (because of their positions as kings) and used it for either monetary or prestigious gain. However, Elijah appears to be motivated more by purpose than by prestige and complies with God's instructions. Also, Elijah knew who Elisha was before Elisha knew who he (Elijah) was and had more insight into Elisha's future then Elisha himself. Elisha had no idea how drastically his life was about the change, and that he was about to encounter his spiritual father, who would set him on an irreversible course for an incredible life and ministry.

When you continue to read and 1 Kings 19, you find that when Elijah finishes his conversation with God, he goes and finds Elisha who was plowing with twelve yokes of oxen before him, and he with the twelfth; and Elijah passed by him and cast his mantle upon him. And he left the oxen and ran after Elijah, and said, "Let me, I pray thee, kiss my father and my mother, and then I will follow thee." And he said unto him, "Go back again, for what have I done to thee?" And he returned from him and took a yoke of oxen and slew them and boiled their flesh with the instruments of the oxen, and gave unto the people, and they ate. Then he arose and went after Elijah and ministered unto him.

It is to be observed that Elisha had the ability to immediately distinguish the difference between his biological father and his spiritual father to be and had no reservation about leaving the former for the latter. No doubt his biological father taught him about the world, however, Elijah would teach him about the kingdom. There also had to be mutual respect between Elijah and Elisha's biological father, because the biological father had no reservations about releasing his son into Elijah's care.

That is the way that it should be, because the relationship between a spiritual father and a son, in the no way supersedes the relationship between the son and the biological father (if there is one and he has been active in the son's life). To the contrary, it is an enhancement of the relationship. If not for the biological father, there could be no spiritual son with which to have a relationship.

One of the greatest honors that I have received was when the biological father of one of my spiritual sons, thanked me for the spiritual impartation that I had made into his son. What I love even the more about it, is that the biological father, in no way feels either minimalize or marginalized by the relationship between his son and I have, and that is the way that it should be.

Just before Elijah is to be taken into heaven (2 Kings 2:1), he is assigned to make one final trip to various cities that he had been influential. He had taught in the schools of the prophets, and his prophetic footprint was in all these places because he had nurtured the prophetic ministries of many. Before Elijah departed for these cities, he asked Elisha to stay where he was, while he went on to the cities. Elisha's answer to Elijah was consistent "As the Lord liveth and as thy soul liveth, I will not leave thee." Also, of every city that they entered the prophets of that city asked Elisha was he aware that Elijah was going to be taken from him. Elijah's was consistent, "Yea, I know it; hold ye your peace."

When you know that everything God is equipping you with for your kingdom assignment is in your spiritual father or mother, you will not allow anything or anyone; to cause you to break the bond that you vowed would be unbreakable. Elijah could not persuade Elisha to stay where he was, and the other prophets could not persuade him to go back to where he left from.

Elisha knew that he had not received from Elijah what he needed to succeed him, and Elijah was about the taken from the earth. From the beginning of their relationship, Elijah and Elisha were inseparable, and to Elisha's credit, he was determined for it to remain that way until the very end. It behooves us to see how this relationship ends, and the picture that it paints of the only way that the bond between parent and child should be broken.

And Elijah took his mantle and wrapped it together and smote the waters, and they were divided hither and thither so that the two went over on dry ground. Everyone else had to view Elijah's departure from their lives, from afar. They had an instructional relationship with Elijah. He taught them much about the prophetic and positioned them to be sons to a father, but not to have any delusions that he was their father. And that is the power of foster parenting; it teaches you how to be the son to the father which is to come.

And it came to pass when they had gone over, that Elijah said unto Elisha, "Ask what I shall do for thee before I am taken away from thee."

And Elisha said, "I pray thee, let a double portion of thy spirit be upon me."

Elisha realizes that if he is to exceed the accomplishments of Elijah, he needs twice as much of what Elijah had to do what he did. Elijah had exemplified before Elisha, a character that no doubt contributed to his ability to do the exploits that he did. Elisha recognizes the power of the right spirit because little can be accomplished for God with the wrong spirit.

Elisha understands that everything that he has become spiritually to this point has been the result of multiple interactions between him and Elijah. So, he has had ample time and opportunity to study the spirit of Elijah, and no doubt considers it a great honor to be endowed with a double portion of his spirit.

Notice Elijah's reply, "Thou hast asked a hard thing. Nevertheless, if thou see me when I am taken from thee, it shall be so unto thee; but if not, it shall not be so." Elijah realizes the magnitude of the request and understands the potential for disappointment if Elisha, does not understand the magnitude of the request.

The potential disappointment works both ways, because if Elisha does not see him when he's taken, undoubtedly, he will be greatly disappointed that he did not get what he was after.

The disappointment for Elijah would be that he was not able to grant the request, because of the inability of Elisha to see him when he is taken, and all the preparation and training would have been for naught.

The disappointment in the son (or daughter) for failing to succeed in his assignment, does not remotely compare with the disappointment of the father (or mother), when he feels that he somehow failed. Because in the mind of the father, the son only failed, because the father failed the son, even if deep within, the father knows that he gave the son everything to succeed. Therefore, Elijah's concern is understandable, due to the magnitude of the request.

And it came to pass, as they still went on and talked, that, behold, there appeared a chariot of fire and horses of fire, and parted them both asunder; and Elijah went up by a whirlwind into heaven. Notice the power of this Scripture. It was heaven that put them together to create the bond, and only heaven could break the bond by taking one from the other. We must understand, that if heaven puts it together, heaven will keep it together, and only heaven should be able to take it apart. Elijah and Elisha walked and talked together until they couldn't walk and talk together any longer.

As much as Elijah did while on the earth, his ultimate performance was what he did in leaving the earth. He shut up the heavens, where there was no rain; he slew 450 prophets single-handedly; he outran horses and extended a meal for two years that was only supposed to last one day. He prayed and brought breath back into a widow's dead son, and as powerful and beneficial as all of that was to the kingdom of God, none of it was his true assignment. His true assignment was to nurture Elisha so that there could be another man in the kingdom of God to carry out God's instructions without fear of reprisal. He was powerful as a prophet, but he was proficient as a father.

Now, he is being taken away from his protégé. And Elisha saw it, and he cried, "My father, my father, the chariot of Israel and the horsemen thereof!" And he saw him no more. And he took hold of his clothes and rent them in two pieces. I can imagine the joy of Elijah when the last glimpse of his son, is enhanced by the last words that he hears from him. Because Elijah's statement to Elisha was that if he saw him when he was taken away that he would get what he wanted had nothing to do with Elijah's geographical position but had everything to do with his relational position.

It wasn't that Elisha had to see him <u>where</u> he was; it was that Elisha had to for <u>who</u> he was. There was absolutely nothing that Elisha could do to change where Elijah was, or even where he was going; however, he could take full advantage of who Elijah was.

That was the difficulty that Elijah saw in the magnitude of Elisha's request. Would Elisha be able to see, why all the years of training? Elijah knew that, if in his departure all Elisha could do was to be despondent or emotional, then he would not have seen what he needed to see. That would have been tragic for both because that would've meant that all the time that they had spent together what have been in vain, because Elisha did not get the point of the relationship. But to Elisha's credit, he got the full impact and the purpose behind their time together, because what he needed to see was that Elijah was his father. Not just his mentor or prophetic teacher, but his father, and he acknowledged this through the utterance of Elijah's name twice. More on this experience will come in a later chapter.

Though not as profound (in miracles) as the relationship between Elijah and Elisha was, the relationship between the apostle Paul and Timothy was unique, nonetheless. Paul, (because of how he comes on the scene) was a very unlikely candidate to become the personification of a spiritual father that he became, primarily because of his initial destructive behavior. So steeped in Jewish tradition was Paul, that not only was he an unlikely candidate to become a spiritual father, he was even less likely to be a candidate for an apostle of Christ.

The thing that separated Paul from all the other apostles was his absolute commitment to his principles. Whatever he sternly believed in, he was committed to faithfulness to, even if it cost him his life. This character trait served him well in his spiritual parenting. Commitment to fulfillment is probably the most necessary ingredient in a spiritual parent/child relationship because it bolsters the confidence of one toward the other. Paul was a spiritual mentor to many. However, his relationship with Timothy stood out above the others. Timothy's youth likely required more hands-on development. It is so important to recognize the character of your spiritual children because it allows you to identify their strengths and weaknesses. Identifying strengths and weaknesses allows one to develop a plan of action to assist the mentee in being successful in his or her assignment.

Paul on many occasions had a contentious relationship with the other apostles (due to doctrinal and personality differences). However, his relationship with Timothy was one of nurturing, instructional, and protection. Paul's letters to Timothy are proof of not only the love that he had for this young man but to his commitment to Timothy's success as a leader as well. Paul not only prepared Timothy for the people; he also prepared the people for Timothy. Paul was held in high esteem by most of the churches that he planted, and it is evident in his letters to the churches (that Timothy would play a leadership role in), that he wanted the churches to hold Timothy in no less esteem.

Paul and Timothy's relationship is similar to the relationship between Elijah and Elisha in this regard; both of the younger men were being trained to be successors of the older men. He makes this statement to Timothy in his second letter to him; "You, however, have followed my teaching, my conduct, my aim in life, my faith, my patience, my love, my steadfastness, my persecutions and sufferings that happened to me at Antioch, at Iconium, and at Lystra—which persecutions I endured." Then he tells him; "continue in what you have learned and have firmly believed, knowing from who you learned it. One reason that Paul could so confidently be at peace with death was that he knew that he had a successor, who knew his way of doing things. Timothy would ensure that those who carried on the work of Paul (including himself), would carry it on the way that Paul did. As with Joshua and Moses, Elisha and Elijah, Timothy knew the ways of his spiritual father, Paul.

One of the most powerful lessons that these successors learned was the way their fathers went before the Lord. They learned not only the power that was derived from their mentors' relationship with God; they also learned the protocol by which they received the power. They were eyewitnesses to the way that their fathers approached the Lord, which was reverentially, but also with confidence. The unbreakable bond between God and their fathers helped to establish an unbreakable bond between them and their fathers. That is the key to an unbreakable bond in all spiritual parent/child relationships.

The adhesive that holds the bond together is communication because regardless of the abilities, or the desire to establish an unbreakable bond, none of it is possible without communication. That is true in all relationships, however. It takes on added significance in a spiritual relationship, because of the critical nature of the assignments involved. Communication is the lifeblood of relationships because it allows the flow of wisdom, strategies, and ideas that ensure that progress is continual.

The level of respect that one has for a relationship can be determined by the degree of communication. One of the most disrespectful things that one can do in a relationship is not returning a communication. A leader is severely handicapped when one of his or her spiritual children does not return a communique whether a phone call, text, email, or letter, because of the inability to relay the content of the need to contact the person. Often information is time sensitive and critical to be relayed instantly. The opportunity is lost when there is a lack of communication.

Those who do not reciprocate a leader's attempt to contact them, do not place value on the relationship and are likely not concerned about an unbreakable bond, and the bond is broken already. When the goal is an unbreakable bond, it is far better to over-communicate than to not communicate, and a leader must never take the position that a little communication is better than no communication at all, because little communication is the next step to no communication.

We must keep in mind the example that we are setting for the faithful sons and daughters. The only plausible and acceptable excuse for not reciprocating a leaders' communique is the absolute inability to do so.

As leaders, we must always be aware, that everything we do is microscopic because someone is always observing our every move. Therefore, we must go to great lengths to protect that which God has entrusted to us.

We are entrusted with the very lives and assignments of people, so every effort must be made to ensure that we are giving them everything that we can. Therefore, it is incumbent upon us to ensure that we do not allow those who are intent on working to create an unbreakable bond, to be compromised by those who have no intent in doing so.

Knowing that communication is the adhesive holding together every other wisdom and strategy in an unbreakable bond, communication must be a requirement that is laid out in setting ground rules.

Chapter 5

The Necessity and the Power of Succession

Though I never met him personally, Dr. Myles Monroe was a great influence in my life and ministry. His book "Rediscovering the Kingdom," revolutionized my understanding of my purpose, more than any other source other than the Bible and the Holy Spirit. It caused me not only to read more of his books but to learn more about him. He was so purposed, and so understood the dynamics of his assignment that death to him was not a sign of failure, but the ultimate acknowledgment of his success.

Shortly before his death, he acknowledged that for all practical purposes, he was empty. Every facet of his kingdom assignment was now in the capable hands of his successors. He had invested years of pouring into the lives of others from the richness of wisdom and revelation that God had deposited into his spirit Everything about Myles Monroe was succession driven because he understood the dynamics and the power of succession. Succession says that the enemy will have no peace from the exposure of his strategies and weaknesses, because of the succession of individuals possessing such knowledge.

The patriarchs of old understood the essence of succession. They realize that for there to be a continuation of what they initiated, there had to be someone in a position to carry it on. That was Abram's dilemma when he talked to God in Genesis chapter 15. God said, "Fear not, Abram, I am your shield; your reward shall be very great." But Abram said, "O Lord GOD, what will you give me, for I continue childless, and the heir of my house is Eliezer of Damascus?" And Abram said, "Behold, you have given me no offspring, and a member of my household will be my heir." And behold, the word of the LORD came to him: "This man shall not be your heir; your very own son shall be your heir."

Abram is caught between the knowledge of the necessity of a successor, and the desire that the successor comes from his loins. His anxieties would have been lessened had he known that God's plan coincided with his desire. We need not ever fear that God's plan for our lives is deplete of a successor. To the contrary, His plan is drawn up with a successor built in, because He understands the power of succession more than we all.

That is why Jesus spent thousands of hours imparting wisdom and strategies into his disciples so that they could succeed Him when His time on earth (bodily) was to be no more. One of the purposes for which he gave the Ephesians 4 gifts to the church was to equip the saints for the work of ministry because this is what he did for his disciples, He equipped them to be his successors so that they could equip others.

Merriam Webster defines succession as the act of getting a title or right, after the person who had that title or right before you, has died or is no longer able or allowed to have it; also: the process by which this happens. That is why we need to understand the gravity of grooming a successor to continue to carry the torch of mentorship when we are no longer able to carry it, thereby guaranteeing the spirit of spiritual parenting will continue.

Everything about this world, and particularly the history of this world is traceable. Everything that we can see can be traced back to something that we can't see, and the kingdom of God is no exception. Everything in life is successive, whether intended or not, everything has succeeded from its source. One of the most successful ministers of our time is Joel Osteen. Lakewood is the largest church in the United States of America, however, even though Lakewood is synonymous with Joel Osteen, and vice versa, the church was founded by John Osteen, (Joel's father).

Joel worked behind the scenes for many years to ensure perfection in his father's ministry, not realizing that God was grooming him to succeed his father. For many years John tried to persuade Joel to preach, only to hear Joel repeatedly decline. Instead, he chose to stay in the background and do whatever necessary to enhance his father's ministry. No doubt John knew all along that he was grooming his successor, even though his successor had no clue.

Joel eventually acquiesced to the will of his father and accepted the invitation to preach, and six days later his father died of a heart attack. Joel began to preach frequently afterward and was installed as the senior pastor of Lakewood that same year. Though not everyone agrees with his theology or methodology, everyone must see in the success that he has obtained, the power of succession. At the apex of John's ministry, Lakewood's membership was 5000; however, under Joel's leadership, the ministry has grown to over 43,000 people.

There is no greater tragedy than to see the leader of a church or organization die, without leaving a successor. What has historically occurred has been chaos due to power struggles. Time and again, great ministries have been reduced to a fraction of what they once were, because of the death of a leader and no successor. Boards of Directors are essential to the operation of ministries and are huge contributing factors to the fulfillment of the vision of the church. However, directors are very rarely successors. A Board of Directors alone cannot hold the vision together when there is no successor to the visionary. That is not to say that they cannot effectively find an interim pastor to fill the void until the permanent replacement can be found.

Most of the time, when that permanent replacement is found and installed, it is usually someone who has been under the mentorship of the leader, even though they may or may not have been designated as a son. Whenever a new leader who was not a part of the original leader takes over a ministry, most of the time the original vision for the ministry is replaced by the vision of the new leader, and the original vision died with the original leader. If a vision is good enough to be given by God to a visionary, that vision is good enough to be successive.

Regardless of how successful a vision that replaces a vision appears to be, if the original vision was not meant to be replaced; how successful is it? There are many things that have the appearance of God, that are not ordained of God, and because they appear to be godly, many times they get buy-in.

Probably the greatest corporate success story in the history of the world is the story of Walmart, and a key contributor to the success of Walmart is that Sam Walton's successors did not deviate from his vision. Many years after his death, Sam Walton's vision is very much alive. One can rarely go anywhere in this country and not find a Walmart close. And even in states that are anti-Walmart, Sam Walton's business model is in play. Love them or hate them, it is very likely that you're going to encounter a Walmart store in your lifetime.

That is one area that the church has missed, and the result is a power vacuum in the church. We have not understood the power of similarity and its role in succession. With few exceptions, if you are familiar with one Walmart, it is not very difficult to navigate through another Walmart even though you've never been to it before. That is because most of them are stocked the same way.

What we have in the kingdom, is this tendency to attempt to mimic the leaders who are in the spotlights, even though we are not sanctioned, sons or daughters. So, there is a lot of mimicking of leaders. However, there is no similarity of spirit, and people have great difficulty trying to navigate through the message.

If we understood, that God places us with that spiritual parent for whom there is to be a similarity, we would find ourselves operating in greater success, because of the embedded power that is in succession. Power to succeed; to forge on through difficulties; power to draw from the wisdom and the knowledge of our God-given spiritual parents.

Every system of God has success built in, and failure omitted. Therefore, if we're not successful, it is because we are not aligned with the system that God has for our lives. God's system from the very beginning has been that each one teaches one so that the message remains fresh and relevant, and he chose to relay it through a family structure. Whether biological or spiritual, the family structure is the foundation of God's system of succession, and that is the reason why the enemy is so opposed to this structure.

The enemy knows that "when" the system of God; (this parenting system,) is carried out the way that God intended, he (the enemy) gets no rest or peace from any generation because the strength of the father is a magnified in the son or daughter.

If we look back over the generations, each generation has produced enhancements of what was originated in previous generations, and most of the enhancements have been for the betterment of mankind. That is no less true spiritually when the hearts of the fathers and the mothers have been knit with the hearts of the sons and the daughters, the children have progressed farther than the parents, by enhancing the knowledge given by the parents.

The enemy has been given a pass for too long because the church got out of the business of succession. It is amazing, that with all the available information and knowledge that this earth possesses mankind remains largely imbecilic in relating this information and knowledge to the kingdom.

Too much of mankind is under the false impression that information, knowledge, and technological advances are produced by a man's intellect and has little or nothing to do with God. Nothing could be farther from the truth; Scripture tells us that what we see, has been made by what we don't see.

The reality is, that everything visible is the result of a revelation from God, on how to construct what we see. That is the information that God deposits in fathers and mothers, to impart into their children so that the knowledge of our Creator is neither lost nor diminished in any generation.

The greatest power in any succession is the knowledge of God. Every father is admonished, equipped, and empowered to pour into his children the knowledge of the existence, will, love and power of God, which is the greatest foundation of every relationship in this universe.

Though we can preach thousands of diverse messages, no message is complete without the knowledge of the attributes of God. That was the message from the first church, and it will be the message for successive church generations because every attribute of God's is filled with Jesus the

Christ. Any message that is depleted of the Lord is not a message from the Lord, and that is a truth that must be instilled in the children in every generation.

Most of the canons of Scripture that we have embraced in Christianity were accepted as canonical Scriptures because of the succession of the stories that were passed down from generation to generation. Without this succession, we would have little to validate what we read. Where physical records have been either scarce or nonexistent, there has always been a successor of some biblically historical personality, who has carried the messages from one generation to the next, which leaves no generation ignorant of the exploits of God.

That is why it is imperative that we become passionate about succession so that we do not rob subsequent generations of the knowledge of and the exploits of God.

The world has become more wicked, and the validity of the Bible is challenged more than ever as to its relevance to this generation. Therefore, it is critical that we do not lose sight of the power of succession.

Every generation is accountable for the next generation, and we cannot leave the next generation in the hands of evil fathers and mothers, and yes even evil spiritual fathers and mothers.

We have been assigned the task of empowering our sons and daughters, to succeed us with the knowledge of the truth, which is found in the word of God, (that shall remain relevant to every generation).

Our willingness to prepare our successors will go a long way toward determining the future of mankind. Some things are eschatologically unavoidable, however not all things are. And since only the Father knows what things are unavoidable, it behooves us to treat all things as avoidable, and seek opportunities to change the minds of generations.

John the Baptizer had one message (the message of repentance), and that one message caused multiplied thousands to change their lives, by changing their way of thinking. That message of repentance continues to resonate, even to this day. John realized that he was a forerunner to the coming of Jesus Christ, (as are we), and our assignment is no less crucial than that of John the Baptist because we likewise are tasked with compelling people to change their thinking.

The word repent is from the Greek word *metanoeō,* which means to change one's mind for better, heartily to amend with abhorrence of one's past sins. If this was the message that John taught to prepare for Christ, and the message that Jesus taught for connection to the kingdom of God, the message is no less relevant for us to teach our sons and daughters, (as well as others that we are exposed to), because this same Jesus is coming again.

With the advent of some of this New Age theology, it is incumbent upon us as spiritual parents, to teach our spiritual children to stand firmly on the foundation of the message that leads people to Christ, and not to themselves as alternatives to Christ.

Scripture is clear, there is but one name given by which man must be saved, and that is the name of Jesus (*Acts 4:12*), and there is no way to the Father except by Jesus (*John 4:6*). That truth must not be allowed to be drowned out by the voices of Pharisaical successors, and New Age philosophers, who not only deny the deity of Jesus but attempt to diminish His relevance as well.

As precious and as fleeting as time is, we dare not waste one conscious moment, in preparing our sons, daughters, and protégés, for the fight of their spiritual lives, due to the enormous and growing amounts of evil influence in this world. Jesus warned us of the craftiness and shrewdness that would perpetuate itself in successive generations when he said the sons of this world are shrewder in dealing with their generation than the sons of light (Luke 16:8).

One has only to look at the penal system in this and other countries, to see the perpetuation of evil instilled from parent to child. Evil is so personified, that it is nothing to see fathers and sons, or mothers and daughters, sharing the penal system and in some cases the same cell.

Sadly, it is also not uncommon to "not see" spiritual children sharing the ministry of the kingdom with their spiritual parents, because neither understood the necessity and the power of succession. If the tide of evil is to be stemmed, it will in large parts be because of the recognition of the necessity and the power of succession in the kingdom.

There are so many more things that could have been accomplished in the kingdom had there been a succession plan. Most assuredly, the world would not be in the condition that it is in, primarily because the succession of the power of the first church would not have allowed the world to drift into its current condition.

No doubt the martyrs who gave their lives for the cause of Christ would be highly disappointed at the state of today's church because it would be so obvious that there was no succession of the commitment to the cause. There appears to be more of a tendency to start something new than to continue something so effective in its origin.

There is now this competitive spirit that has invaded the church, causing a practice of outdoing one another, for the sake of fame, fortune, and peer accolades. To them, it necessitates creating something new and going all out to draw people to it. There is this quest for the crowds, to receive validation from the other leaders who have "made it," and the only purpose that sons and daughters serve is to enrich the reputation of the leader.

On numerous occasions, I've heard leaders bragging about the number of spiritual children they had, while at the same time observing little to no spiritual growth in any of the spiritual children.

From the ambiance of the sanctuary and the home of the leader, it was abundantly clear that the children had poured greatly (particularly financially) into the leader, without obvious reciprocation from the leader.

That is tragic, because it is the responsibility of the leader to pour into the child so that they might become empowered to progress in every facet of life, and out of the gratitude of the child, the leader will be blessed. Invariably, there was always at least one spiritual child who sees this as the path to success and strives to emulate it, and far too often branch out and create the same monstrosity.

Succession occurs one way or the other; however, it is more beneficial for the kingdom when succession is deliberate. Accidental succession is when one is emulated without input into the life of the emulator.

Fascination with style and methodology has caused more accidental succession than deliberate succession. That is why this book is in some way a call to arms because we cannot afford to allow one more generation of accidental succession that can cause irreparable damage to God's system of succession. They don't succeed the leader whom they emulate; they succeed in becoming copies of the leader without any personal, relational bond.

The more ammunition that we give the enemy, the more dangerous he becomes, and the minimizing of the effectiveness of the kingdom become more of a reality than we care to admit.

Now I know that there will be many who will say that this could never happen, however I can assure you that there were many who if told that prayer would be taken out of school; that abortion could become the law of the land, as well as same-sex marriage, would have said that it could never happen either. As of this writing, all of them are a reality in this country.

The complacency of the church has done more to stymie the flow of the power of God to prevent evil, than the ingenuity and the strategies of the enemy to permeate it. No truer quotes have ever been made than those of Edmund Burke.

He said that "the only thing necessary for the triumph of evil is for good men to do nothing.' In Burke's letter to William Smith, he wrote: "nothing is so fatal to religion, as indifference." As profound as these statements are, there was one statement that he made that should either indict or ignite the believer in Christ. It should also serve as a catalyst for renewing the hearts of leaders to become passionate about equipping their spiritual children with the power to be difference makers, and world changers in that their generation. Burke states, "There is nothing that God has judged good for us, that he has not given us the means to accomplish, both in the natural and moral world."

We are without excuses for not accomplishing the assignments that God has given us for this world. We have been empowered not only by the revelation of who He is, but we are also endowed with the power of his Spirit, whereby we may declare with the Scripture, that greater is He that is within us, than he that is in the world (1 John 4:4). This assurance, of the indwelling of the greater One, must be passed on to successive generations, so that we are raising spiritual giants, and not be left with spiritual dwarfs.

Needless to say; the replication that comes as a result of the succession is worth all the effort that went into the preparation. Because, it ensures the father that the vision of the success of the son or daughter, will not die and subsequent generations will benefit from the same system of succession.

How many times have we witnessed a small child stepping into their father's shoes and trying to walk in them? It is as if there is this built-in desire to not only fill out the shoes but to walk in them in the same manner that they have seen their father walk.

In the same manner, spiritual parents must carry themselves in a way that the child has no greater design your than to fill the shoes of his or her parent and walk in that same manner of godly character. That is the consummate manner of succession. Even Jesus said that "I only do what I have seen the father do (John 8:38)."

Chapter 6

Discerning the Release Point

When I worked in corporate America, one of the questions that could be expected in any interview process was, what are your strengths and weaknesses. Even when opportunity areas were substituted for weaknesses, the question was fully understood. My strength has always been that I am a developer of people and that has served me well over the years. When the question turned to weaknesses or areas of opportunity, without hesitation, my answer has been, "knowing when to let go."

When your life is consumed with the success of others; one of the most difficult things to admit is that you cannot help everyone. That is one of the primary reasons for wasted time on lost causes, and one of the unforeseen casualties in this is that the ones who can truly benefit from the relationship, are deprived of the time.

We must realize that just because a person might be a lost cause with you, does not mean that they are a hopeless case; more than likely the relationship was never meant to be. That is why (as mentioned in a previous chapter), the God factor is so critical in establishing and maintaining relationships.

Early in 2014, I was overwhelmed with the reality of being made in the image of God, and every message that I preached, in some way included this reality.

One of the things that the enemy has done well has been to cause us to focus on our disfigurements, which causes us to forget that we are made in the image of the Creator of all things. It was God's choice to make man in his image, and who knows better how to maintain that image, than God?

I bring this out because of how imperative it is that we never lose sight of this truth because that is the only way that the enemy can cause one to focus on what God did not make. Sin may have marked us. However, sin did not make us; God did.

We have been stained by the things that we've done that were not pleasing to God. However, we must keep in mind that what we did, was, and never will who we are; we have always been God's creation.

Now if we always bear in mind that we are made in the image of God, it behooves us always to seek to do things the way that God does, and to know things the way that God knows them. In doing so, we get the results that He got. It was necessary to bring that out so that we know "when" the relationships are supposed to be.

God gives us assurances in the relationships that are carried on according to His way of relating. The "a clause" of 2 Timothy 2:19 says that God's firm foundation stands, bearing this seal: "The Lord knows those who are his," so if God knows who he is, then we should know who ours are. Another example of assurance that the Lord has, that we should also have, is John 10:14 when he said "I am the good shepherd. I know my own, and my own know me."

Jesus was not only skilled in carpentry; he was a master builder of men. He built through precept and example while establishing strong relationship simultaneously. An overlooked character of Jesus was his ability to blend diverse personalities into an apostolic unit. The 12 disciples in Jesus's inner circle had more differences than similarities, yet the Lord blended them and caused them to recognize that their strength was in their unity.

True spiritual father and spiritual mothers will invariably be faced with a multitude of diverse personalities because like moths drawn to a flame, children are drawn to the earnestness of true spiritual fathers and mothers. That is why it is so important to know those who truly are assigned to your life, as well as you to theirs, because to not know, can have devastating effects.

We must keep in mind, that the most valuable asset we have is time. Therefore, it is essential to exercise time management, because wasted time can never be recaptured, and whatever or whomever the time was wasted on, was to the detriment of other things or people who could have benefited from it.

We must also bear in mind, that though God gave us dominion over the earth, He did not give us dominion over one another. Therefore, we must always be conscious of the fact that every spiritual relationship has a time factor involved. The time that we have with spiritual children as leaders is limited, therefore it is essential to maximize.

Regardless of how many spiritual children you might have, your time with them is limited, and there comes a time that they must be released into their destinies.

The parent/child relationship and bond should last a lifetime. However, the preparation for destiny has an expiration date, and one of the strengths of a true leader is discerning when that time comes.

I have not only witnessed others victimized by leaders unwilling to release them into their assignment, I too have been a victim of such, and one of the things that I vowed to do, was never to be a leader that would deliberately hold a son or daughter back, when it was time for them to be released. Romans 8:19 says, for the creation waits with eager longing for the revealing of the sons of God. Though the context of this Scripture is different, I saw something in it that was relevant to the necessity of releasing a son or daughter when it is time for them to go. I cannot help but consider the possibility that the sons of God are not being revealed, because of not being released by those who have oversight of them.

As leaders, we must in no way feel diminished at the release of a spiritual child. To the contrary, we should be elated because the kingdom of God is being equipped with another leader that is ready to raise other leaders to deflate the already defeated kingdom of the devil.

The more children one releases, the more capacity one has for others. As important as it is to discern the precise time to release a spiritual child, it is equally important to guard against children who are not ready, though they might think that they are simply because a brother or a sister is being released into their destiny. That is one of the most delicate areas in spiritual parenting because sibling rivalry is not only an occurrence in the world; it is also alive and well in the kingdom.

That is also why it is so important to lay a solid spiritual parenting foundation and set ground rules from the onset. That helps to avoid a tenure mentality. By that, I am referring to a spiritual child thinking that they are ready to leave because they have been with you longer than the others.

Those coming to you must understand that everyone comes in with different levels of experiences, needs, learning abilities, and different assignments. That is not to say that one assignment is more important than the other; one assignment might be needed sooner than the other.

All assignments come from God and He not only knows what assignment is needed. He also knows when it is needed. Whenever God is at the forefront of every decision, it tends to lessen the adverse receptions of the decision.

Whenever a leader's ministry experiences exponential growth, the invariable consequence is a deluge of potential sons and daughters. With this deluge comes the necessity of being more corporate in parenting, because it is virtually impossible to give every son and daughter individual time.

The Bible tells us in Luke chapter 10 that there were 70 other disciples besides the 12; however, it was the 12 that comprised his inner circle. However, the 70 were not deprived of His tutelage, because they were given a very similar charge as the 12, to announce the kingdom.

We can see this in Scripture, because Luke 9:1 says and he called the twelve together and gave them power and authority over all demons and to cure diseases, and he sent them out to proclaim the kingdom of God and to heal. And he said to them, "Take nothing for your journey, no staff, nor bag, nor bread, nor money; and do not have two tunics. And whatever house you enter, stay there, and from there depart. And wherever they do not receive you, when you leave that town shake off the dust from your feet as a testimony against them." And they departed and went through the villages, preaching the gospel and healing everywhere.

That was the charge that he gave the 12, let's look at the charge he gave the 70 in the next chapter. Carry no moneybag, no knapsack, no sandals, and greet no one on the road. Whatever house you enter, first say, 'Peace be to this house!' And if a son of peace is there, your peace will rest upon him. But if not, it will return to you. And remain in the same house, eating and drinking what they provide, for the laborer deserves his wages. Do not go from house to house. Whenever you enter a town, and they receive you, eat what is set before you. Heal the sick in it and say to them, 'The kingdom of God has come near to you.' But whenever you enter a town and they do not receive you, go into its streets and say, 'Even the dust of your town that clings to our feet we wipe off against you.

Though the 70 spent less individual time with Jesus, they were no less equipped than the 12, because Jesus equipped them all for their assignments. It is also to be noted that the 12 were not envious of the 70, neither was the 70 envious of the 12. Jesus does something so powerful with the 70 because He knew that they were not his successors. However, He did know that they would be his witnesses.

I believe that Jesus makes the following statement to the 70 so that they would not feel less important than the 12, at the point of succession. He says to them (when they return with such excitement that the demons were subject to them through His name), "I saw Satan fall like lightning from heaven. Behold, I have given you the authority to tread on serpents and scorpions, and over all the power of the enemy, and nothing shall hurt you. Nevertheless, do not rejoice in this, that the spirits are subject to you, but rejoice that your names are written in heaven." He's saying to them in such a wise way; that, even though you will not have the notoriety of the 12, you will be empowered to continue your work, and be fortified therein.

You may not go to the same places as the 12, but wherever you go you will go with authority, and you will not be harmed. Though no one through history will know your name, be content in knowing that I know your name and that your name is written in heaven. What a marvelous way to prepare a group (that has interconnected through a leader), for the advent of a release into a profound destiny for some in the group; but not all. And to do so by creating excitement within the group that would not receive the notoriety of the others (and not even deem it necessary to do so), because they had received their accolades from the leader.

When knowing when to let go is taken in proper context, it is always seen as a strength and not a weakness. It can also be the catalyst for either longevity or premature demise. To let go when it is time to do so can minimize adverse effect on either on one's physical health or mental health, which itself promotes longevity. However, to hold on to what should be let go of, can have the opposite effect. That is why most edible or drinkable products have expiration dates on them. If you consume them within the time before the expiration date, they can be of great benefit; however, to consume them after the expiration date can be quite detrimental to one's health.

I happen to be one who believes that every accomplishment of man, whether technological, literary, agricultural, scientific or any other method of advancing humanity, is inspired by God, for good. Admittedly, often, what God has inspired for good, has been transformed and used for evil, and what was meant to better humanity has hurt humanity; however, God's original intent remains. So, the use of expiration dates is an inspiration from God to help safeguard our health Needless to say; if God knows how to safeguard our health through product dating, He certainly knows how to safeguard our health in relationships. It is not the fault of God if we extend the intent of the relationship beyond its expiration date, and consequently suffer harm.

It must never be forgotten that God is omniscient. He not only knows all things, but he knows all things well, and it would be to our advantage to keep our ears open to His leading. Though God put emotions in us, He did not do so for us to either lead or be led by emotionalism. Our emotions are given to us so that we might remain people of his character, and act upon the needs of one another through God's instructions.

We are to be empathetic and sympathetic to our brothers' causes. However, we're not to feel sorry for them, because feeling sorry leads to complacency, and even hopelessness, but rarely does it spur one to action.

For years, I saw homeless people and felt sorry for them, when I saw them; however, not long after departing their presence, I gave little thought to their plight. It took the word of God to spur me into action. I didn't just read what Jesus said in Matthew 25:42; I heard what He said. In this passage of Scripture, He said: "I was hungry, and you gave me no food, I was thirsty, and you gave me no drink, I was a stranger, and you did not welcome me, naked and you did not clothe me, sick and in prison and you did not visit me."

From the day that this Scripture registered in my heart, I vowed within myself, and to the Lord, that whenever I was exposed to an opportunity to help my brother; I would do all that I could' to do so. I am a man of great compassion, and I am very empathetic and sympathetic to the hurts of this world, but most importantly, I am a man of action.

That is why it is so important to discern the timing of the release because just possibly, the world is being deprived of assistance' because I continue to hold on to the one who has been assigned to assist the world.

When we truly understand, that what God assigns belongs to Him, we will become better at hearing Him when it is time to embrace, and eventually, let go. In Solomon's discourse in chapter 3, he says, that there is "a time to embrace and a time to refrain from embracing." The beauty of it all, is that we don't have to figure out the time, because God already knows it, and if we would but trust him, the personification of Romans 8:28 would lend itself to the cause, and we can have the assurance that all things will work together for good. We must remember that those who are being released love God and are called according to his purpose.

The most painful part of releasing is due to the time, love, and labor that goes into the relationship. There is this emotional attachment that is very difficult to let go of because the leader knows that he has invested a part of himself into the child, and it can seem as if in releasing the child, it somehow depletes you of that part of you. To the contrary, every void that God allows, He refills and equips you to be able to invest twice as much of yourself into the next one to be released. Every released child does so much more than the last released child and becomes a force, too mighty for the enemy's plans.

The stench of staleness is so overpowering that it makes its way through the entire house, and rooms that should contain other fragrances; now bear the scent of staleness. Staleness comes from something that should have long since been released. Whether we pay attention to the expiration date or not, staleness will make itself known, and cause attention to it, that could have been devoted elsewhere.

That is what happens when we hold on to that spiritual child, that was ready to be released. They become stale, and their odor permeates the ministry. Before you know it, children that should emit other scents, now bear the scent of that stale brother or sister.

The thing about an odor that is not dealt with is that eventually, one becomes adjusted and immune to the odor, and the stench is not as pronounced. The problem is, that though the odor is lightly detected from the inside, it is greatly recognized from the outside, and opens the door for many opportunities, of which most are not good.

When those scavengers from the outside, can dictate the staleness of one of your spiritual children, it opens the door for them to offer an alternative to your ministry, that can not only be attractive to the stale one but to the others that the scent is on as well. Often, before you can detect it, your ministry is not only in disarray but potentially in demise. Now you're left with the reality that the assignment that you were given is now in the hands of another who is ill-equipped to carry it out, and your children are in the hands of a cruel stepparent that will abuse them at every opportunity.

Please understand, this is in no way an indictment against stepparents because some stepparents have contributed more to the successes of their stepchildren than their biological parent ever did. The analogy used is in comparison to those stepparents who have contributed more to the detriment of their stepchildren than the biological parent. It is to help us get a better grasp understanding the necessity of timely to release.

There are few things more frightening than entering into new relationships. I am sure that many can attest to the dread of moving to another city. Whether it is to start a new job, attend a new school, or something else. The dread is having to interact with people whom you've never known before. The mind is inundated with thoughts of acceptance, and the possibility of rejection.

Many times, this has caused such anxiety that people have become physically ill at the thought of building new relationships. That is whether previous relationships were either good or bad. If the previous relationships were good, there is a tendency to think that the new relationships cannot measure up, and if the previous relationships were bad, the tendency is to think that the new relationships will either be more of the same or worse.

What we must keep in mind with spiritual parenting is we're always going to be faced with new spiritual children; that, for the most part, are coming out of previous relationships. That is why it is so critical to know them that labor among you.

Ground rules should always consist of making newcomers feel welcome, and for the other children not to pry into the previous lives and experiences of the newcomer. Information gathering should be the responsibility of the parent. However, this is not to say that the other children are not to be alert to tendencies, and behaviors that the newcomer exhibits, particularly if they are detrimental to the well-being of all.

The parent must be wise enough, and know their children well enough, to know when an area of concern about the newcomer, is valid or made up because the one who is expressing his concern, is doing so out of fear (or in many cases jealousy). They might feel that the newcomer will take some of the attention away from them. We must keep in mind, that often those who come to us for a spiritual parent/child relationship, are sometimes immature and insecure, and that is why they need the spiritual parent. Now there are those who seek your parenting because they have discerned that you have what they need to get them where they know that they are supposed to be.

One of the primary areas that a leader must excel in is in the area of recognition. A leader must recognize what he or she is working with, because it goes a long way in getting peer assistance, and that helps the leader establish his or her parental foundation.

You must recognize from the beginning those who come to you with a similar spirit, because they can be you by proxy, among their peers, when you cannot physically be present. Believe it or not, those who come to you with similar spirit as yours, are very rarely the first to leave, to the contrary, they are usually the very last to leave. That is in large part because they understand the necessity of assisting you, with the development of those that are being prepared to embark on their assignments.

They did not come with their mind on leaving at the soonest possible moment; they came to stay until the very last moment, and to assist in whatever way they can, as well as to learn from you all that they can. These are the ones, who most likely succeed you after you're gone, because of the familiarity that they had with your vision, as well as the familiarity that those in your ministry have of them. So, they too must be very carefully guarded about when to release, because there is this tendency to want to launch them because of their faithfulness to you, and you send them into areas that they have no desire to be. Many times, they do not have success in these areas, because their place was and is with you. There is nothing wrong with rewarding faithfulness; however, the reward must be kept in perspective, with the assignment of the one rewarded.

The more efficient a leader becomes in discerning release time; the more efficient the totality of his or her ministry becomes, because of the enablement of utilizing the various skill sets among the spiritual children. Everyone has something to offer; the challenge is discovering what others have to offer. In doing so, the experiences that we can gain from the interaction and the exchanges of ideas, and strategies, are innumerable. Granted, a multiplicity of personalities can be challenging. However, they can also be extremely rewarding, when learning to mesh him.

One of the most successful professional basketball coaches in history is Phil Jackson. Phil won a total of 11 NBA championships with two different teams and a variety of different players. He utilized what is called the "triangle offense," with both teams. Though he had what is called superstars on both teams, the role players were just as significant to the success of the teams, as were the superstars. His success was not due solely to the triangle offense, because one of his assistant coaches got a head coach opportunity, and used the triangle offense, and failed miserably.

It is not so much Phil Jackson's ability to coach the triangle offense that made him so successful as a coach; it was his ability to take a group of players with very distinct and strong personalities and to get them to play together as a unit. To witness the behavior of some of these players off the court, one would never think that they could work within a system. There had to be an embrace, of not only of diversification of a skill set to adjust to a different system, but there also had to be a diversification of personality, to adjust to playing with different personalities, of which many were opposite.

God created such diversity in humans, that no two share the same fingerprints, or the same eye patterns, or even the same DNA (unless identical twins), so there should always been expectation of having to interact with different (and sometimes extremely different), personalities. This way, when you are confronted with different personalities, it is no surprise.

The challenge then is to develop a strategy that meshes the personalities, to operate in a system. When we do this, it helps tremendously to enhance our ability to discern the proper time, to either release those that are ready to go, or those in whom you cannot benefit. Because we cannot benefit some, it does not mean that someone else cannot.

Therefore, it is incumbent upon us not to waste unnecessary time in trying to; and simultaneously deprive the one who can benefit from the time that they need for you to spend with them. Once a leader masters release times, they are ready for the joy of accomplishment.

Chapter 7

The Joy of Accomplishment

Most of my tenure in corporate America was in a sales' environment. Every job that I spent at least six months on; through the favor of God, I always had the privilege of being promoted to management positions. I had numerous opportunities to be a part of the development of training modules, and systems testing. These training modules and systems were developed to maximize the ability of the sales force to be successful.

Numerous studies have been done on "what motivates salespeople," and the obvious conclusion that one would draw is that it is money. However, most studies have shown that the most successful salespeople are not necessarily motivated by money alone; most of them are motivated by recognition. I worked some years for a very large corporation and found that our most successful salespeople truly were motivated by the recognition that they received for their success, more than they were by the money.

People who have never worked in a sales environment have no idea of the stress level that this environment produces. Regardless of how successful one is in any given month, in most cases the next month, one starts at zero sales, and the necessity to produce starts all over again. The money is usually good for successful salespeople. However, there is one frequent occurrence, and that is that money is spent, and when it is gone, it can no longer be used to validate one's success.

There is one thing that is always a testament to success, and that is the method of recognition, whether a plaque, certificate, trophy, or some of the memento, to show that you did it, and you know that the display of your success, is there to be witnessed not only by your peers but for your motivation as well. A job well done, produces the joy of accomplishment; it could be said that it is the fruit of one's labor. There are few things as satisfactory as knowing that you not only finished your assignment, but that you finished it well.

This same joy of accomplishment occurs when one of our spiritual children goes out and establishes the foundation for his or her ministry. The success of their ministries creates an entirely different sense of joy than one's success. The mere fact that they took the tools that their spiritual parent equipped them with and embraced the challenge of initiating the ministry in which their assignment would be known by creates a euphoric sense of accomplishment that is difficult to compare.

Many of us have experienced the honor and the joy of seeing our biological children finish their academic levels and walk across the stage in cap and gown to receive their certificate, diploma, or degree. As euphoric as that moment was, far too many parents have been put in the unenviable position of seeing the same child make a conscious decision to doing nothing with the academic experience they received.

The relationships between the spiritual parents and children often exceed biological relationships, unless they are the same, for there are times, that a leader has the distinct privilege of being a spiritual father or mother to a biological child. That is especially the case when the biological child desires to continue with his or her biological parent in a spiritual capacity.

Too often, biological children have no desire to continue in a spiritual capacity, because of all the undue, and too often unfair expectations, that have been placed upon them most of their lives, by sometimes well-meaning, and far too often unwise parishioners. Somehow, much of the body has ascribed to this philosophy that the children of leaders are not allowed to be children, and everything that they do, though similar (if not exact) to the content of other children; is often met with contempt, ridicule, or outright scorn. That is why many leaders are deprived of the privilege of being succeeded by those of their household, especially when they have the potential and often the abilities to do so.

The joy of accomplishment can be such a catalyst in impassioning a leader to extraordinary heights and developing the others in the fold, because the euphoria that accompanies a successful release of a child, never gets old.

True leaders are driven by the possibilities of their children exceeding his or her every accomplishment in life and ministry. That should always be the joy that accompanies one's achievements in life. However, the joy of one's own success should always be exceeded by the joy of the success of another, when the Lord allowed him are her to be a part of that success.

As previously mentioned, it is a poor parent who does not desire that their children achieve more in life than they did, primarily, because successive generations have more in their generations with which to be challenged.

True parents never want their children to be victimized by the pitfalls of which they (the parents) were victimized. They have no desire for their children to repeat the self-destructive decisions that they made, often because of the severity of the consequences of the decision.

Every spiritual relationship should start with a celebration of success in mind. In doing so, failure is not an option, because success is the goal. There is this adage in business that should be remembered in the spiritual relationship, and that is if you fail to plan; you plan to fail. The more excited that we are about guiding our children to a successful conclusion, the more plausible our plan appears to them, and we must keep in mind the likelihood of them emulating our personalities.

If we're honest about it, most of us have fragments of those who have impacted our lives through the influence that they've had in our lives. And, who we are, in addition to our individualities, are fragments of their personalities.

How often have we found ourselves not only repeating what we heard from either our fathers/mothers or other spheres of influence but repeating it in the same mannerisms in which they spoke? Those who do not understand the significance of those relationships, many times mistakenly attribute our actions to trying to mimic those influences in our lives.

In cases of authentic relationship, it is rare that we were deliberately trying to be like them; however, because of the magnitude of the influence and contributions that they made in our lives, it was unavoidable for the similarity not to show up in our lives.

It is no small honor for me to see myself in one of my spiritual children and realize that it is not a conscious decision that they're making to resemble me in speech and mannerisms. It was an unavoidable consequence of the time spent in the process of them getting to that point. I have shared many laughs with some of my spiritual children, when they have reported back to me, they found themselves in speaking situations, saying some of the things that they've heard me say in some of the meetings, that they have supported me in.

These are the times when the joys of accomplishment are at their best. These are the times when you look back over time spent in the process and realize that it was worth every second, regardless of how difficult some of those times were.

There is no greater agony for a true leader, then to see their child in agony, whether from financial and marital difficulties, deaths, and many other adverse situations. When they hurt; you hurt. The process, many times is like a seesaw that goes up and down. The preference is always to be up. However, the reality is that there are down moments, and sometimes numerous down moments. The challenge is not to allow the down moments to define the process and realize that ups and downs are not exclusive to a spiritual process, but a reality of life.

For this reason, is to be understood, that the purpose of the process is to mold the assignment, to minimize the downs, and maximize the ups. The call of God on the lives of our spiritual children is not just to expose sin, but to expose the kingdom of God as well, so that a loving Savior can be revealed, as the only source to make this world better. The better the world, the less opportunity for those downs.

There are few places in the Bible, that exhibit God's preponderance for completion than found in Isaiah 46:10 – 11. He announces himself in verse 9 as God, and begins first 10 with; declaring the end from the beginning, and from ancient times things that are not yet done; saying, My counsel shall stand, and I will do all my pleasure; calling a ravenous bird from the east, the man of my counsel from a far country; yea, I have spoken, I will also bring it to pass; I have purposed, I will also do it.

That is so powerful because he seems to reverse time. He is so conscious of the finish that He takes the end from the beginning so that completion is always present. By taking the end from the beginning, He does not eliminate the beginning; He places it where the end was so that when the process is completed, it is reunited with the beginning, which inaugurates the purpose for which the process was all about. Oh, the depth of the riches and wisdom and knowledge of God! How unsearchable are his judgments and how inscrutable his ways (Romans 11:33, ESV)!

We see how incredibly kind God is to us when we scrutinize how He so strategically plans the process. He does not alert us to the pitfalls and the dangers that He leads us through because He knows that by doing so, the propensity of us saying no, could potentially sabotage the destinies of those whom He has given us oversight. Also, to say no would deprive us of the exhilaration that comes from the successful completion of the process. That shows the magnanimity of His agape because even in the concealment of some of the process, His desire is for the parent and the child to experience the joy of completion.

Some of the greatest things that the Lord does for us are things that we are unaware that He is doing. The element of faith is so relevant in this truth, because of the awareness that it brings; that we must trust Him always.

We must trust Him when we are believing for a favorable outcome, because we have an awareness of what He is doing, and we must trust Him, even when we either don't have a clue what He is doing, or when we are not aware of Him doing anything at all.

I have concluded that because I don't always know what He is doing, does not mean that he does always know what He is doing, because He always does. We must take God at his word, and we must take His word, like Him. To take every Scripture that references God's preponderance for completion and quote them would merely make this book another Bible, and that is not my intent. However, I do deem it necessary to include certain Scriptures, because to not do so, would leave no biblical foundation for which to build on.

There are two verses in Psalms 126, that though they are talking about the planting of seeds, they are so relevant to this discussion, because we deposit seeds of greatness, through the inspiration of the Holy Spirit, into the lives of our spiritual children, and as previously mentioned; it is sometimes a tearful process. Verses five and six of Psalms 126 class that, those who sow in tears shall reap with shouts of joy! He who goes out weeping, bearing the seed for sowing, shall come home with shouts of joy, bringing his sheaves with him.

The consolation of the parent should be, that no matter what God requires of us to deposit into our children, He provides, and He has an inexhaustible supply. For that reason, we should never feel that we will not have enough, regardless of how much we give.

There are times that it takes an enormous amount of effort to ready a child for his or her assignment, and granted, that can be exhausting. However, the supply of effort is inexhaustible, because it comes from God. Though the exact number of Hebrews that were freed from Egypt is not known, most theologians, biblical scholars, and historians place the number at several million people.

There is an episode in Exodus where God quenched the thirst of the entire population from a rock. It does not say from a mountain but a rock. The transliteration of rock is *"tsuwr"* which means, a block of stone, boulder.

The point of this is that God can supply the water to quench the thirst of millions of people from a rock, certainly, He can supply the necessities of the process of grooming our spiritual children for their assignments. Therefore, we must never allow the difficulties in raising some, to overshadow God's ability to replace everything that was exhausted n the difficult process.

The joy of accomplishment in the difficult process is no less exhilarating, than the joy that accompanies the less difficult processes. There are times that the joy of accomplishment of the difficult processes, far exceed the joy of the less difficult, because of the numerous obstacles that were overcome to complete the process.

For those who have experienced spiritual parenting, there is the awareness that we are not privileged with the information as to the tenure of the process, we only know that it begins, and for that reason, we should always be committed to the duration; whatever the duration.

We also know, that we can never expect for the tenure of the process, to be the same for all of the spiritual children, however, we can expect the joy of accomplishment to be the same, if not exceeding. It is good to remember, that often, the more one puts into the process, the more one can expect for the joy of accomplishment, to equal the input, if not exceed the input altogether.

True spiritual parents are not the least apprehensive about giving all they have for the development of their children and have the wisdom to give the rest to God. When we give the rest to God, in His infinite wisdom, He gives us rest, and then re-deposits what we gave Him, and does so in a way, that we think that it is something fresh.

The only reason for our selection for the process of spiritual parenting is that God knows that he has equipped us to do so and would by no means expect anything from us that we are unequipped with.

The challenge is, to not be so overwhelmed by the assignment, that we make false assumptions in the assignment, that cause us to exceed the boundaries of our equipping. For in doing so, we run the risk of blaming God for our failures and feeling abandoned by Him because of feeling that He should have assisted us in our efforts.

We need to keep in mind, that God is not obligated to either influence or interfere in matters that He did not initiate because He knows that what he initiates. He has the responsibility to equip. The blessing that we enjoy, is that so often His mercy offsets our mistakes, ignorance, and sometimes arrogance, and covers us, even though He does not have to. Because He did not initiate what caused us to fail, however, we must not take His mercy for granted, because we should be led by the Holy Spirit and not our proclivities.

The Holy Spirit will never lead us in a path that God has not already forged and navigated for us, so if we find ourselves in failure, we must quickly realize that we are off course, and if we are off course, so are our children. The Lord told us in Jeremiah 29:11 that He knows the thoughts that He has for us, thoughts of peace, and not of evil, and to bring us (by His Spirit) to an expected end, and the joy of accomplishment is encapsulated in that end, because God rightfully takes pleasure in His accomplishments.

What we must take from this, is that if we align our thinking with God's way of thinking, then regardless of the potential for difficulty, we face the process with thoughts of peace, and not of evil, and the expected end will result in joy.

There is one aspect of God that is often taken for granted and it is one of the most critical aspects of Him. as it relates to human design, and that is that God does not create anything unnecessary.

Everything in man's physical makeup is a representation of God's character. Though God is Spirit, the Bible gives references of physical characteristics when relating to God, such as the eyes of God; ears of God; hands and mind of God, etc. That is so that we understand that God knows everything that we experience in the physical, and can identify with it, however, it cannot affect Him, in the same manner, that it affects us.

What God does revelatory, is to expose us to spiritual remedies for physical ailments, and He does so by directing us to our original state, which is His image. Whenever our mind accepts that we are made in the image of God, it becomes quite difficult to be persuaded to either allow or accept an alternative image. The reason that I am reinforcing the mental aspect of spiritual parenting is that true sons and daughters are after our mental reflections of God.

True sons and daughters on never after the material gains of the father, there are seeking the father's conceptualization of God, because that is the essence of the father. No one seeks God in someone who has no concept of who God is. It stands to reason, that if one has not found God, doubtless he can lead someone else to God.

Whatever the level of wisdom that the son or daughter enters the relationship with, that wisdom leads to the understanding that the enhancement of the child will come from the father's experiences with God. The wonderful thing about experiences with God is that; not only does it heighten the expectations of the next encounter with God; it also broadens the imagination as to the prospects of God, because of the unlimited power and the wisdom of God.

When Solomon was put in the unenviable position of reigning over the United Kingdom of

Israel at such a young age, he knew that to discharge his duties faithfully, that he needed God's help. His request of God and second Chronicles 1:10 was Lord "give me now wisdom and knowledge to go out and come in before this people, for who can govern this people of yours, which is so great?" That has been my prayer my entire ministry.

Though Solomon was speaking numerically and experientially, I habitually echo this prayer, because of the awareness of the incredibly gifted and anointed people that the Lord has allowed me to spiritually father. Because of the incredible and sometimes frightening responsibility of pouring into the lives of those who I have discerned from the onset of the relationship, will far exceed anything that I've done in ministry or otherwise. It is essential that I pray for wisdom. My consolation in knowing that those true sons and daughters would far exceed my exploits is that I wouldn't have it any other way.

As much as I love all my sons and daughters, and the interactions and, the camaraderie that we share, I do not lose sight of the fact that one day their greatness will not allow them to stay at this level of relationship. The demand for the anointing on their lives and the purpose for which they are anointed will be greater than their desire to sit at the feet of their father. They will have to sit in their seats, so that their children can sit at their feet and be nourished by the wisdom and God experiences that they have received.

Rest assured those days are filled with dual emotions. On the one hand, there is this sadness because of the difficulty of releasing your spiritual child into their destinies. On the other hand, there is this joy of accomplishment. That is because you have that assurance that not only are they are ready to embark upon their destiny but that the God who assigned the destiny, will ensure the success therein.

The blessing of the joy of accomplishment is that it is continual. Every time your spiritual child experiences another victory over some challenge in their ministry, the joy is rekindled. The relationships that derive from true spiritual parenting are lifelong. Though the child leaves the fold, he or she never leaves your heart, prayers, or thoughts. And, they have the assurance that you will always be there for them, and they will always be there for you, and for their spiritual siblings, whether in the fold, or have launched into their own destinies.

Conclusion

One of the greatest causes of the breakdown in our society has been the breakdown in the church. The very first chapter in the Bible and the very first verse makes us aware that before there was anything else, there was God, and if there was God, there was godliness. Before there was a war in heaven, there was harmony and bliss in heaven. When Lucifer sought to disrupt the godliness of heaven, he was cast out of heaven, because disorder is never the will of God. That is why everything that He does is designed to either maintain or establish order. He knows, that where there is order, there is the fruit of the Spirit, love, joy, peace, patience, kindness, goodness, faithfulness, gentleness, self-control, and where the fruit of the Spirit is, He is honored.

He cannot be very pleased with the state of the world, and if the world is a reflection of the church; He cannot be very pleased with the church. A dysfunctional world can only be possible, because of a dysfunctional church. The reason being, according to the apostle Paul and second Corinthians 5:18, we have been given this ministry of reconciliation. Reconciliation comes from the Greek word *katallagē,* which means adjustment of a difference, reconciliation, restoration to favor; in the NT of the restoration of the favor of God to sinners that repent and put their trust in the expiatory death of Christ.

What we are faced with, is not the fruit of the Spirit, but the works of the flesh, which are sexual immorality, impurity, sensuality, idolatry, sorcery, enmity, strife, jealousy, fits of anger, rivalries, dissensions, divisions, envy, drunkenness, orgies, and things like these. The tragedy in all of this is that these works of the flesh are projected in the church proportionately to their projection in the secular world. The world is in a grave state of disorder, and the only possible solution to the restoration order is to awaken the body of Christ from its slumber and refocus the people of God on their assignments. The only way that this will occur is that the hearts of the leaders are renewed, and spiritual parenting again becomes a priority.

With few exceptions, every generation is the result of the continuation of the previous generation. There is a saying that is quite common in our environment, and that is, "if you want to know why a child behaves a certain way in public, follow them home." The implication is that the child is emulating what he or she is witnessing at home. There was a time in years past, that there was some validity in this statement, however, beginning in the latter part of the 20th century, there was this inundation of independent spirits, and rebellion against authority, that was rare prior to that point, and the child is not always a reflection of the parent.

At one time, the United States of America was a model for decency and morality, however,

114

after every decision to acquiesce to the will of man by successfully eliminating God and/or His godliness from this society, we have been met with a noticeable decline in morality, respect for authority, and fellow man. The apathy of the body of Christ, not only allowed the rights of God to be trampled on, we have also allowed ourselves to become marginalized, ridiculed, and pushed almost to the point of irrelevance. That is the result of a false sense of security that the church was too powerful, to ever be relegated to its current state.

Ironically, every time that the church is faced with defeat, the inclination is always to pray for recovery, however, rarely does a church come together and pray for insight, which will lead to prayers of prevention. God blesses purpose at the initiation of it because He is the one who initiates it. He knows not only what the purpose is, but also for what it is purposed. He initiates prayers of prevention because He knows what the obstacles are, that confront purpose. Prayers of recovery, however, are initiated by us, because we have been confronted by unexpected defeats, and are left scrambling for answers.

When we initiate prayer, we must wait for answers, however, when God initiates prayer, there are no questions, because He's given insight into what the confrontation will be, and how to defeat it. God never delays an answer when the question concerns His will, there was only a delay at the imposition of our wills, whether knowing our unknowing.

That is why it is so important that the hearts of the fathers are turned to the sons and the daughters. The only hope that we have is that a generation of God-fearing and God believing man and women of God are nurtured into a place, that the sons and the daughters that the whole creation has been waiting in anticipation are revealed.

It is imperative that the men and women of God who have been spiritually parented, began to mentor their sons and daughters to be unapologetically "apologetic." So that they not only denounce the false biblical teachings and practices, that are so prevalent in the body of Christ right now, (which is one of the primary reasons for the negative perception that the world has of the church), but also to present Jesus Christ, in a way that He becomes irresistible to the world.

To remain status quo is to make the church and all things God, unattractive, however, to change, which is, in essence, to be renewed to our former glory, that came as a result of our being made in the image of God, will assuredly make God, and all things God irresistible.

This book was not written to be the final authority on spiritual parenting, and I by no means am purporting to present myself as having the only insight into this needed subject. I am merely sharing years of insight and experience in hopes of spurring leaders to action and fulfill our roles of spiritual parents to a much-needed group of ministers who are void of such.

I pray that there are others who have more insight into spiritual parenting will come forth and allow us to benefit from your insight so that we can reposition the church to the respectability that we see in the book of Acts.

I also want to thank the readers of this book for allowing me the privilege of engaging your time to read it and my prayer is that the time spent was beneficial. I solicit your prayers as I continue this journey to keep the church relevant in these chaotic times that we are in.

God Bless You

www.ingramcontent.com/pod-product-compliance
Lightning Source LLC
Chambersburg PA
CBHW051835040426
42447CB00006B/543